Deutsch...

...auf Englisch!

A German language textbook
for first-year students at Japanese universities

Tobias Bauer

英語で学ぶドイツ語

著者： Tobias Bauer　熊本大学准教授

表紙イラスト：犬塚千裕
吹込：Svea Pries, Marcel Boye
写真提供：p. 25: Andreas Schwarzkopf, p. 95: Thomas Wolf (1-3), Michael Chlistalla (4), Thomas Doerfer (5) (Wikipedia Commons, CC-BY-SA 3.0)

Preface

Learning a second foreign language is an integral part of the curriculum in most Japanese universities. As an important part of general education, second foreign languages are thought to provide students with the necessary communication skills to survive in an increasingly globalized society and broaden their perspectives by introducing them not only to the language but also to the culture, thought, and history of non-English-speaking countries.

German courses at Japanese universities normally use textbooks written in Japanese to introduce students to basic German grammar and develop the four basic skills (listening, speaking, reading and writing), with either German or Japanese used as the classroom language. Although this method is part of a long, successful tradition, it is the intention of this textbook, "Deutsch auf Englisch," to try a new approach. It differs from previous textbooks in that it makes intensive use of students' existing skills in English by introducing and discussing various aspects of German grammar and giving instructions for exercises and vocabulary use exclusively in English. Furthermore, this textbook also taps students' hitherto-accumulated knowledge of the English language, particularly grammar, in the belief that the knowledge and experience of studying English can boost their acquisition of German language skills. Being a historically and linguistically close relative to German, English is thought to serve as both a tool of grammatical comparison and a foundation upon which the differences and characteristics of the German language can be viewed more clearly.

This idea is represented in the double meaning of the title of this textbook, "Deutsch auf Englisch." The title's first meaning refers to the concept of studying "German in English," that is using English instead of Japanese as the textbook (or even classroom) language. This is based on the English language's growing importance as a means of global communication. Without detouring through the mother language of Japanese, this textbook offers students a more direct access to the German language and allows them to gain experience and confidence in using English as a means of communication.

The second meaning of the title represents the premise that studying "German based on English," (that is, using previously acquired English knowledge to learn the sister language of German) is a promising approach. Since both languages share common roots and a good part of their vocabularies, the knowledge of English not only fosters the acquisition of German but also helps deepen one's understanding of the English language and the system of European languages in general.

Tobias Bauer

Contents

Preface		1
Contents		2
Lesson 0	**Basics**	5
	(1) The German Alphabet, (2) Pronunciation, (3) Numbers, (4) Greetings	
Lesson 1	**Introductions**	9
	Dialogue: Mein Name ist Florian.	
	Grammar: (1) Personal Pronouns, (2) Verbs: Present Tense (Regular Verbs), (3) Verb Placement, (4) Verbs: Present Tense (Irregular Verb: *sein*)	
	Vocabulary: Basic Verbs	
Lesson 2	**Directions**	17
	Dialogue: Wo finde ich die Universität?	
	Grammar: (1) Gender of Nouns, Definite and Indefinite Articles, (2) Agreement of Third-person Pronouns (Singular), (3) Declension of Nouns: The Four Cases (Nominative, Genitive, Dative, and Accusative), (4) Verbs: Present Tense (Irregular Verbs: *haben* and *werden*)	
	Vocabulary: Basic Nouns 1	
Lesson 3	**Shopping**	25
	Dialogue: Eine Ansichtskarte kostet zwei Euro.	
	Grammar: (1) Noun Plurals, (2) Declension of Plural Nouns, (3) Declension of Weak Nouns, (4) The Numbers 0-100	
	Vocabulary: Basic Nouns 2	
Lesson 4	**Hobbies and Preferences**	32
	Dialogue: Was ist eigentlich dein Hobby?	
	Grammar: (1) Verbs: Present Tense (Irregular Verbs), (2) Imperative, (3) Personal Pronouns (Dative, Accusative)	
	Vocabulary: Irregular Verbs	
Lesson 5	**Transportation**	39
	Dialogue: Wo bekomme ich eine Fahrkarte?	
	Grammar: Prepositions I (Prepositions Taking the Genitive, Dative, or Accusative), (2) Prepositions II (Two-Way Prepositions), (3) Contraction of Prepositions and Definite Articles, (4) *Da*-Compounds	
	Vocabulary: Basic Nouns 3	
Lesson 6	**Invitations**	46
	Dialogue: Dazu habe ich keine Lust.	
	Grammar: (1) *Der* Words, (2) *Ein* Words, (3) Negative Sentences Using *nicht* and *kein*, (4) Numbers 100 and Above	
	Vocabulary: Basic Nouns 4	

Lesson 7	**Visits**	53
	Dialogue: Darf ich dir etwas anbieten?	
	Grammar: (1) Modal Verbs, (2) Future Tense	
	Vocabulary: Basic Nouns 5	
Lesson 8	**Health**	61
	Dialogue: Ich fühle mich schlecht.	
	Grammar: (1) Verbs with Separable Prefixes, (2) Verbs with Inseparable Prefixes, (3) Reflexive Verbs	
	Vocabulary: Reflexive Verbs	
Lesson 9	**Past Experience**	69
	Dialogue: Ich war schon einmal in Frankreich.	
	Grammar: (1) The Three Basic Verb Forms: Infinitive, Past, and Past Participle, (2) Simple Past, (3) Subordinating Conjunctions and Subordinate Clauses	
	Vocabulary: Verbs with Separable Prefixes	
Lesson 10	**Recent Events**	76
	Dialogue: Ich bin nach Japan geflogen.	
	Grammar: (1) Present Perfect, (2) Uses of *es* as a Subject, (3) Infinitives with *zu*	
	Vocabulary: Basic Nouns 6	
Lesson 11	**Appearances**	82
	Dialogue: Tolle Party, nicht wahr?	
	Grammar: (1) Usage and Declension of Adjectives, (2) Comparison of Adjectives	
	Vocabulary: Basic Adjectives 1	
Lesson 12	**Procedures**	90
	Dialogue: Zuerst werden die Kartoffeln gekocht.	
	Grammar: (1) Passive Voice, (2) Stative Passive (*Zustandspassiv*), (3) Relative Pronouns and Relative Clauses	
	Vocabulary: Basic Nouns 7	
Lesson 13	**Dreams**	97
	Dialogue: Ach, wäre ich doch Millionär!	
	Grammar: (1) Subjunctive II	
	Vocabulary: Basic Adjectives 2	
Supplement	(1) Verbs: Present Tense (Regular Verbs) - Exceptions, (2) Interrogative Pronouns *wer* and *was*, (3) Contraction of Prepositions and Interrogative Pronoun *was* (*Wo*-Compounds), (4) Adjectives as Nouns, (5) Ordinal Numbers, (6) *Wer* and *was* as Relative Pronouns without Antecedents, (7) Passive of Intransitive Verbs, (8) Subjunctive I, (9) Demonstrative Pronouns, (10) Present Participle, (11) Expression of Years	103
Appendix I	**List of Common Irregular Verbs**	107
Appendix II	**List of Grammatical Terms**	111

All audio files 🔊 01 are available for download at http://www.dogakusha.co.jp/onsei.html.

Deutsch auf Englisch Lesson 0 - Basics

Lesson 0 - Basics

Basics 1 - The German Alphabet 🔊 01

A a	*A a*	aː		Q q	*Q q*	kuː
B b	*B b*	beː		R r	*R r*	ɛʁ
C c	*C c*	tseː		S s	*S s*	ɛs
D d	*D d*	deː		T t	*T t*	teː
E e	*E e*	eː		U u	*U u*	uː
F f	*F f*	ɛf		V v	*V v*	faʊ
G g	*G g*	geː		W w	*W w*	veː
H h	*H h*	haː		X x	*X x*	ɪks
I i	*I i*	iː		Y y	*Y y*	ˈʏpsilɔn
J j	*J j*	jɔt		Z z	*Z z*	tsɛt
K k	*K k*	kaː				
L l	*L l*	ɛl		Ä ä	*Ä ä*	ɛː
M m	*M m*	ɛm		Ö ö	*Ö ö*	øː
N n	*N n*	ɛn		Ü ü	*Ü ü*	yː
O o	*O o*	oː				
P p	*P p*	peː		ß	*ß*	ˈɛstsɛt

5 - fünf

Deutsch auf Englisch — Lesson 0 - Basics

Basics 2 - Pronunciation 🔊 02

- Basic rules of spelling and pronunciation:
  - German pronunciation is similar to that of Japanese "rōmaji".
  - In general, the first syllable of a word is stressed. However, loanwords are stressed on their last syllable.
  - (Stressed) vowels are long when they are followed by a single consonant or by *h*. They are short when followed by two or more consonants.
  - All German nouns are capitalized.

some examples: **Náme** *name*, **kált** *cold*, **Blúme** *flower*, **kúrz** *short*,

Appetít *appetite* [loanword], **Momént** *moment* [loanword]

1) Vowels 🔊 03

1.1) Modified Vowels (Umlauted Vowels)

①	ä	[ɛː][ɛ]	**Bär**	*bear*	**Kälte**	*cold*
②	ö	[øː][œ]	**schön**	*beautiful*	**öffnen**	*to open*
③	ü	[yː][ʏ]	**müde**	*tired*	**Hütte**	*hut*

1.2) Diphthongs

①	ei	[aɪ]	**drei**	*three*	**arbeiten**	*to work*
	ay, ey		**Bayern**	*Bavaria*	**Meyer**	*[last name]*
②	eu, äu	[ɔʏ]	**heute**	*today*	**läuten**	*to ring*

1.3) Long Vowel

①	ie	[iː]	**lieben**	*to love*	**wieder**	*again*
		[iə]	**Famílie**	*family*	← when the *ie* is not stressed	

2) Consonants 🔊 04

①	-b, -d, -g	when ending a word: [p], [t], [k]	**Lob**	*praise*	**und**	*and*
			Tag	*day*		
②	-b, -g	when preceding -s or -t: [p], [k]	**Obst**	*fruit*	**sagen → sagt**	*to say*
③	vowel + -h	A vowel followed by -h is long.	**gehen**	*to go*	**wohnen**	*to live*
④	j	[j]	**Japan**	*Japan*	**Jahr**	*year*

⑤	s	[z] (in front of vowels)	Suppe	soup	sollen	should
		[s]	Kunst	art	Haus	house
⑥	v	[f]	Vater	father	viel	a lot of
		[v] (mainly loanwords)	Klavier	piano	Violine	violin
⑦	w	[v]	Wagen	car	Wort	word
⑧	z, tz	[ts]	Zimmer	room	jetzt	now
	ts, ds		rechts	right	abends	in the evenings
⑨	ch	[x] (when preceded by a, o, u, or au)	Nacht	night	hoch	high
			Buch	book	auch	as well
		[ç]	ich	I	Kirche	church
⑩	chs, x	[ks]	sechs	six	Examen	examination
⑪	-ig	[ıç] (as a word ending)	lustig	happy	König	king
			however: [g]→		Königin	queen
⑫	pf	[pf]	Apfel	apple	Pfarrer	pastor
⑬	qu	[kv]	Quelle	spring	bequem	comfortable
⑭	r	[r] [ʀ]	rot	red	rauchen	to smoke
		word ending -er [ɐ]	Bier	beer	Mutter	mother
⑮	sch	[ʃ]	Schule	school	Schwester	sister
⑯	sp-	[ʃp]	spielen	to play	spät	late
⑰	st-	[ʃt]	stehen	to stand	Stuhl	chair
⑱	ss (following a short vowel)	[s]	essen	to eat	müssen	to have to
	ß		heißen	to be called	grüßen	to greet
⑲	th, dt	[t]	Theater	theatre	Stadt	town
⑳	tsch	[tʃ]	Deutsch	German	Kutsche	coach
㉑	ti	loanwords from Latin: [tsi]	Nation	nation	Operation	operation

Deutsch auf Englisch   Lesson 0 - Basics

Basics 3 - Numbers 🔊 05

0	null	15	fünfzehn	30	drei**ß**ig
1	eins	16	**sech**zehn	40	vierzig
2	zwei	17	**sieb**zehn	50	fünfzig
3	drei	18	achtzehn	60	**sech**zig
4	vier	19	neunzehn	70	**sieb**zig
5	fünf	20	zwanzig	80	achtzig
6	sechs	21	**ein**undzwanzig	90	neunzig
7	sieben	22	zweiundzwanzig	100	[ein]hundert
8	acht	23	dreiundzwanzig	200	zweihundert
9	neun	24	vierundzwanzig	1 000	[ein]tausend
10	zehn	25	fünfundzwanzig	10 000	zehntausend
11	elf	26	sechsundzwanzig	100 000	hunderttausend
12	zwölf	27	siebenundzwanzig	1 000 000	eine Million
13	dreizehn	28	achtundzwanzig		
14	vierzehn	29	neunundzwanzig		

378	dreihundert | achtundsiebzig
4 659	viertausend | sechshundert | neunundfünfzig
23 456	dreiundzwanzigtausend | vierhundert | sechsundfünfzig
789 234	siebenhundert | neunundachtzigtausend | zweihundert | vierunddreißig

Basics 4 - Greetings 🔊 06

Hallo!	*Hello!* (infml)	**Guten Appetit!**	*Enjoy your meal!*
Guten Morgen!	*Good morning!*	**Danke!**	*Thanks.*
Guten Tag!	*Hello!*	**Danke schön!**	*Thank you very much.*
Guten Abend!	*Good evening!*	**Vielen Dank!**	*Thank you very much.*
Gute Nacht!	*Goodnight!*	**Bitte (schön)!**	*Please! / You're welcome. / Here you are.*
Grüß Gott!	*Hello!*		
	(Austria/Southern Germany)	**Wie geht es Ihnen?**	*How are you?*
Auf Wiedersehen!	*Goodbye!*	**Wie geht's?**	*How are you?* (infml)
Tschüss!	*Bye!* (infml)	**Danke, sehr gut / gut / es geht /**	
Servus!	*Hello! / Goodbye!*	**nicht so gut.**	
	(infml; Austria/Southern Germany)		*Thank you, very good / good / it's ok / not so good.*
Einen schönen Tag!	*Have a good day!*		
Bis bald!	*See you soon!*	**Entschuldigung!**	*Excuse me. / I'm sorry.*

Lesson 1 - Introductions

Dialogue - Mein Name ist Florian. 🔊 07

- Hallo, ich heiße Anna. Und wie heißt du?
- ◇ Mein Name ist Florian.
- Wie bitte? Noch einmal bitte!
- ◇ Florian. F-L-O-R-I-A-N. Florian ist mein Vorname und mein Familienname ist Schneider.
- Freut mich, Florian. Kommst du aus Deutschland?
- ◇ Ja, ich komme aus Berlin.

heiße **heißen** *to be called*
und *and*
wie *how*
mein *my* (possessive adjectives ⇒ Lesson 6 Grammar 2)
r **Name, -n** *name*
ist *is* **sein** *to be* (⇒ Grammar 4)
r **Vorname, -n** *first name*
r **Familienname, -n** *family name*
Freut mich. *Pleased to meet you.*
kommen *come*
aus *from*
ja *yes*

Classroom Communication 🔊 08

Wie bitte?	*Sorry?*
Bitte nicht so schnell!	*Not so fast, please.*
Ich verstehe nicht.	*I don't understand.*
Ist das richtig?	*Is this correct?*
Noch einmal bitte!	*Once again, please.*
Wie schreibt man das?	*How do you spell that?*
Wie heißt das auf Deutsch?	*How do you say that in German?*
Wie heißt ... auf Japanisch?	*What is ... in Japanese?*

Deutsch auf Englisch — Lesson 1 - Introductions

Grammar 1 - Personal Pronouns

		English	German
singular	first person	I	ich
singular	second person	you	du
singular	second person	you	Sie
singular	third person	he	er
singular	third person	she	sie
singular	third person	it	es
plural	first person	we	wir
plural	second person	you	ihr
plural	second person	you	Sie
plural	third person	they	sie

➢ In German, there are two sets of pronouns corresponding to the English *you*: the informal *du* (singular) and *ihr* (plural) and the formal *Sie*, used for both the second-person singular and plural; in other words, it can refer to either one person or to several people.

   Michael, hast **du** Hunger?   *Michael,*
   Kinder, habt **ihr** Hunger?   *Kids,*   } *are you hungry?*
   Herr Müller, haben **Sie** Hunger?   *Mr. Müller,*
   Herr und Frau Müller, haben **Sie** Hunger? *Mr. and Mrs. Müller,*

➢ *Du* and *ihr* are used to address family members, relatives, friends, and acquaintances who are called by their first names as well as children and animals. They are also commonly used between college students, members of the same sports teams, etc. *Sie* is the form of address used for strangers or people not close enough to be called by their first names.

   Martin, lernst **du** Deutsch?   *Martin,*   } *do you study German?*
   Herr Wagner, lernen **Sie** Deutsch?   *Mr. Wagner,*

➢ *Sie*, the formal *you*, is always capitalized. On the other hand *ich* is always lowercased (except at the beginning of a sentence).

   Heute fahre **ich** nach Berlin.   *Today I go to Berlin.*
   Ich lerne Deutsch.   *I study German.*

➢ Be careful: A lowercased *sie* corresponds to the English words *she* and *they*. At the beginning of a sentence, a capitalized *Sie* can mean *she*, *they*, *you* (formal, singular), or *you* (formal, plural). The correct meaning can be identified through the context and/or the verb form (⇒ Grammar 2).

                                          ***They** live in Berlin.*
   Sie wohnen in Berlin.   { ***You [formal, singular]** live in Berlin.*
                                          ***You [formal, plural]** live in Berlin.*

   Sie wohnt in Berlin.   ***She** lives in Berlin.*

> Unlike the English *it*, things or ideas are referred to by not only *es*, but also by *er* or *sie* depending on the gender of the antecedent (⇒ Lesson 2 Grammar 2).

Grammar 2 - Verbs: Present Tense (Regular Verbs)

		English	German
infinitive		(to) learn	lernen
stem			lern
singular	first person	I learn	ich lern**e**
singular	second person	you learn	du lern**st**
singular	second person	you learn	Sie lern**en**
singular	third person	he / she / it } learn**s**	er / sie / es } lern**t**
plural	first person	we learn	wir lern**en**
plural	second person	you learn	ihr lern**t**
plural	second person	you learn	Sie lern**en**
plural	third person	they learn	sie lern**en**

> While English verbs (with the exception of *be*) only have two present-tense forms (*learn, learns*), German present-tense verb forms change from person to person. Changing the form of a verb to make it agree with the subject of a sentence is referred to as conjugation. Note that the forms *Sie*, *wir*, and *sie* take the same ending as the infinitive (*-en*). Furthermore, *he/she/it*, and *ihr* also share the same ending (*-t*).

> German verbs in their infinitival form (their basic dictionary citation) end in *-en* (or in some cases *-n*). The part without the infinitive-ending *-en/-n* is called the stem.

    infinitive/dictionary form: kommen   stem: komm   *(to) come*
    infinitive/dictionary form: wohnen   stem: wohn   *(to) live*
    infinitive/dictionary form: angeln   stem: angel   *(to) fish*

> German verb conjugations take the stem as the starting point and add an ending that agrees with the person of the subject.

    gehen [*(to) go*] → geh → du geh**st** [*you go*]
    machen [*(to) do*] → mach → sie mach**en** [*they do*]

> Since all regular verbs are conjugated as shown in the table above, it is advisable to memorize these endings as the standard conjugation pattern: e-st-t-en-t-en (as the endings for *ich*, *du*, *er/sie/es*, *wir*, *ihr*, and *sie*; the ending of *Sie* is identical to that of *sie*).

> For exceptions to this conjugation pattern, refer to ⇒ Supplement 1.

Deutsch auf Englisch — Lesson 1 - Introductions

Grammar 3 - Verb Placement

Verb as the second element in the sentence		
declarative sentence	Er **lernt** jetzt Deutsch.	*He is learning German now.*
	Deutsch **lernt** er jetzt.	*He is learning German now. {It is German, that he is learning now.}*
	Jetzt **lernt** er Deutsch.	*Now he is learning German.*
interrogative sentence containing a question word	Was **lernt** er jetzt?	*What is he learning now?*
Verb at the beginning of a sentence		
interrogative sentence without a question word	**Lernt** er jetzt Deutsch?	*Is he learning German now?*

➤ In basic German sentences (those consisting of only one clause), the verb is either placed in the second position or at the beginning of the sentence, depending on the type of sentence.

➤ "Second position" does not necessarily means the second word in a sentence but rather the second informational unit.

<u>Nach der Schule</u> **esse** ich eine Pizza.   <u>*After school*</u> *I eat a pizza.*

➤ In interrogative sentences without question words, the verb (position 1) is followed by the subject (position 2).

➤ Conjunctions such as *aber* (*but*), *denn* (*because*), *oder* (*or*), and *und* (*and*) do not change the word order of the sentences they precede.

Ich lerne Deutsch, <u>aber</u> er **lernt** Englisch.   *I am learning German,* <u>*but*</u> *he is learning English.*

Grammar 4 - Verbs: Present Tense (Irregular Verb: *sein*)

infinitive	sein (to be)	
	singular	plural
first person	ich **bin**	wir **sind**
second person	du **bist**	ihr **seid**
	Sie **sind**	Sie **sind**
third person	er / sie / es **ist**	sie **sind**

Ich **bin** Student.   *I **am** a student.*
Er **ist** reich.   *He **is** rich.*

Deutsch auf Englisch Lesson 1 - Introductions

> ➤ Together with *haben* and *werden* (⇒ Lesson 2 Grammar 4), *sein*, the equivalent to English *be*, is one of the most important irregular verbs in German, so it should be memorized. It is also used as an auxiliary verb for building the present perfect (⇒ Lesson 10 Grammar 1).

Politeness in German

In German, the level of politeness is not just indicated by the use of the personal pronouns *du* and *Sie*; the correct use of greetings and the proper use of names when addressing others is equally important.

(fml) **Guten Tag, Herr Meier, woher kommen Sie?** *Hello Mr. Meier, where do you come from?*
　　formal greeting + *Herr* (Mr.) / *Frau* (Mrs.) [family name] + *Sie*
(infml) **Hallo, Martin, woher kommst du?** *Hi Martin, where do you come from?*
　　informal greeting + [first name] + *du*

Question Words 🔊 09

wann *when*	**warum** *why*	**was** *what*
wer *who*	**wie** *how*	**wo** *where*
woher *where from*	**wohin** *where to*	

German Proverbs – deutsche Sprichwörter (1)

Aller Anfang ist schwer.

All beginnings are difficult.

Deutsch auf Englisch   **Lesson 1 - Introductions**

Exercise 1 【Grammar 2】

Fill in the correct form of the verb given in ( ).

① Was _____ du? (studieren) *What do you study? (What is your major?)*
② Ich _____ gern Apfelsaft. (trinken) *I like to drink apple juice.*
③ _____ ihr morgen auch zur Party? (kommen) *Will you also come to the party tomorrow?*
④ Wir _____ deutsches Essen. (lieben) *We love German food.*
⑤ Sie _____ sehr schön. (singen) *She sings very well.*

Exercise 2 【Grammar 1,2,3,4】

Fill in the personal pronoun and verb in their correct order and form.

① Wo _____ _____, Frank? - Ich wohne jetzt in Aachen. *Where do you live, Frank? - I live in Aachen now.*
② Sind Sie Amerikaner? - Nein, _____ _____ Kanadier. *Are you American? - No, I am Canadian.*
③ _____ _____ auch Japanisch, Herr Schuster? - Nein, ich lerne Chinesisch. *Do you study Japanese as well, Mr. Schuster? - No, I study Chinese.*
④ Trinkt ihr gern Wein? - Ja, aber _____ _____ lieber Bier. *Do you like to drink wine? - Yes, but we prefer to drink beer.*
⑤ Woher kommen sie? - _____ _____ aus München. *Where do they come from? - They come from Munich.*

Exercise 3 【Question Words】

Select the answer from the right hand column that best completes the question on the column on the left ①-⑧. Also, memorize the German question words (⇒ page 13).

① Wie heißen Sie?   •   •   Aus Deutschland.
② Wohin fahren wir morgen?   •   •   Ich bin krank.
③ Wo wohnt sie?   •   •   In Bonn.
④ Warum kommst du heute nicht? •   •   Das ist Florian.
⑤ Was studiert ihr?   •   •   Ich heiße Schmidt.
⑥ Wann spielen wir Tennis?   •   •   Nach München.
⑦ Wer ist das?   •   •   Wir studieren Germanistik.
⑧ Woher kommst du?   •   •   Morgen.

> **fahren** *to travel,* **morgen** *tomorrow,* **wohnen** *to live,* **studieren** *to study,* **nach** *to,* **Deutschland** *Germany,* **krank** *ill,* **Germanistik** *German language and literature / German studies*

Deutsch auf Englisch — Lesson 1 - Introductions

Speaking Exercise 1 【Grammar 2, Basic Verbs】

Practice the conjugation of regular verbs by using the verbs on ⇒ page 16. Take turns to choose a verb. Roll a dice to determine person and number and then read the correct form aloud.

⚀	ich	example:	**ich winke** *I wave*
⚁	du	example:	**du stehst** *you stand*
⚂	er / sie / es	example:	**er / sie / es rennt** *he / she / it runs*
⚃	wir	example:	**wir fragen** *we ask*
⚄	ihr	example:	**ihr spielt** *you play*
⚅	sie	example:	**sie malen** *they paint*

Speaking Exercise 2 【Basics (1) The German Alphabet】 🔊 10

Practice the following dialogue with your partner. Use your own names in the parts underlined.

● Guten Tag. Darf ich mich vorstellen? Ich heiße <u>Andrea Schneider</u>.
◇ Guten Tag, <u>Frau Schneider</u>. Mein Name ist <u>Murakami</u>. Ich komme aus <u>Japan</u>.
● Wie bitte? Buchstabieren Sie bitte!
◇ <u>M-U-R-A-K-A-M-I</u>. Und mein Vorname ist <u>Daisuke</u>.
● Freut mich, Sie kennenzulernen, <u>Herr Murakami</u>!

> **Darf ich mich vorstellen?** *May I introduce myself?*
> **Ich komme aus ...** *I come from ...*
> **buchstabieren** *to spell*
> **Buchstabieren Sie bitte!** *Please spell it!* (imperative ⇒ Lesson 4 Grammar 2)
> **Freut mich, Sie kennenzulernen!** *Pleased to meet you!* (infinitives with *zu* ⇒ Lesson 10 Grammar 3)

German Proverbs – deutsche Sprichwörter (2)

Anfangen ist leicht, Beharren eine Kunst.

Starting is easy, persistence is an art.

Deutsch auf Englisch

Lesson 1 - Introductions

Objectives

In this lesson you have learned how to

- ✓ greet people
- ✓ introduce yourself
- ✓ communicate in the classroom

Vocabulary - Basic Verbs 🔊 11

1 **winken** *to wave*
2 **stehen** *to stand*
3 **rennen** *to run*
4 **fragen** *to ask*
5 **spielen** *to play*
6 **malen** *to paint, to draw, to color*
7 **zeigen** *to point, to show*
8 **springen** *to jump*
9 **trinken** *to drink*
10 **sitzen*** *to sit*
11 **weinen** *to cry, to weep*
12 **grüßen*** *to greet*
13 **schaukeln** *to swing*
14 **rutschen** *to slide*
15 **klettern** *to climb*

All verbs above are conjugated according to the rules for regular verbs introduced in ⇒ Grammar 2. For verbs marked by * refer to ⇒ Supplement 1.

Lesson 2 - Directions

Dialogue - Wo finde ich die Universität?

🔊 12

● Entschuldigen Sie bitte, wo finde ich die Universität?

◇ Die Universität? Die ist nicht weit. Gehen Sie hier geradeaus und dann rechts.

● Vielen Dank. Ach ja, und wo ist denn hier ein Café?

◇ Gleich hier links.

● Danke schön.

---

finden *to find*
e **Universität, -en** *university*
Die = Die Universität (demonstrative pronoun ⇒ Supplement 9)
nicht *not*
weit *far*
gehen Sie *go* (imperative ⇒ Lesson 4 Grammar 2)
hier *here*
geradeaus *straight ahead*
dann *then*
rechts *right*
ach ja *oh, (I just remembered / one more thing)*
denn [modal particle marking questions of interest / making the question sound less direct - no consistent translation; here: *oh, by the way*]
s **Café, -s** *café*
gleich *right, just, immediately*
links *left, on the left*

Gender of Nouns - How to Read the Dictionary

Your dictionary provides you with important information for using nouns correctly. It includes not only their gender but also plural forms and declensions. Make sure to familiarize yourself with the dictionary you are using.

*das **Ba·by** [ベービ béːbi] [英] 中 (単2) -s/(複) -s ① 赤ん坊, ベビー. Sie erwartet ein *Baby*. 彼女は身ごもっている. ② 《口語》 頼りない人; (愛称として:)かわいこちゃん.

In this example taken from a Japanese dictionary (『アポロン独和辞典』、第3版、同学社), the gender of *Baby* is neuter as indicated by the preceding article *das* and the symbol 中 (⇒ Grammar 1). "単2" refers to the genitive ending of the noun, indicating that the ending *-s* has to be added: *des Babys* (⇒ Grammar 3). Finally, the plural form is given by "(複)-s", showing that again the ending *-s* is needed: *die Babys* (⇒ Lesson 3 Grammar 1).

Deutsch auf Englisch — Lesson 2 - Directions

Grammar 1 - Gender of Nouns, Definite and Indefinite Articles

➢ Capitalization is not the only way in which German nouns differ from English nouns. German nouns also have "grammatical gender"; that means they are classified as masculine, feminine, or neuter. Gender is indicated by the article preceding the noun.

	definite article + noun	indefinite article + noun	examples of indication of gender in dictionaries and vocabulary lists
masculine	**der** Vater [*the father*]	**ein** Vater [*a father*]	男 / m. / der / *r*
	der Tisch [*the table*]	**ein** Tisch [*a table*]	
feminine	**die** Mutter [*the mother*]	**eine** Mutter [*a mother*]	女 / f. / die / *e*
	die Tasse [*the cup*]	**eine** Tasse [*a cup*]	
neuter	**das** Kind [*the child*]	**ein** Kind [*a child*]	中 / n. / das / *s*
	das Foto [*the picture*]	**ein** Foto [*a picture*]	

➢ Note that the grammatical gender does not necessarily match biological gender. For example, while *das Kind* could refer to either a male or female child, its grammatical gender is always neuter. Another example is the neuter *das Brüderlein* [*the little brother*], referring to a male person.

➢ Although rules exist to determine the gender of a noun (e.g., most nouns ending in -*e* are feminine), in the beginning, it is advisable to memorize each noun together with its definite article as a set or use color markings to indicate the gender of a noun in your vocabulary list or on your flash cards (e.g., blue for masculine nouns, pink for feminine nouns, and yellow for neuter nouns).

➢ The gender of compound nouns is determined by the gender of the final component.

   das Haus + **der** Eingang → **der** Hauseingang

   [*the house + the entrance → the entrance of a house*]

➢ While in English, grammatical gender is reflected only by pronouns (*he, she, it*) and possessive pronouns (*his, her, its*), in German, gender is indicated not only by pronouns, nouns, and articles but also by adjectives (e.g., *eine schöne Frau, ein schönes Kind*, ⇒ Lesson 11 Grammar 1)

➤ German article usage parallels the English distinction between definite articles for referring to specific or already known entities and indefinite articles for referring to new information or unspecific or unknown entities.

Grammar 2 - Agreement of Third-person Pronouns (Singular)

English			German
This is the father. **He** is tall.	he	er	Das ist der Vater. **Er** ist groß.
This is the mother. **She** is nice.	she	sie	Das ist die Mutter. **Sie** ist nett.
This is a table. **It** is small.	it	er	Das ist ein Tisch. **Er** ist klein.
This is a cup. **It** is red.		sie	Das ist eine Tasse. **Sie** ist rot.
This is a picture. **It** is old.		es	Das ist ein Foto. **Es** ist alt.

➤ Personal pronouns match the respective grammatical gender of the antecedent (the person, thing, idea, etc. they refer to).

➤ Note that in German, masculine and feminine third-person pronouns are used to refer to not only people but also replace things and ideas. Therefore, the German *er* and *sie* both correspond to the English *it* when they refer to things or ideas.

Grammar 3 - Declension of Nouns: The Four Cases (Nominative, Genitive, Dative, and Accusative)

➤ In German, nouns, articles, pronouns and adjectives can occur in four different cases, corresponding to their function in a sentence: nominative (words used for the subject), genitive (words indicating possession), dative (words indicating an indirect object), and accusative (words indicating a direct object).

➤ Nouns, articles, pronouns, and adjectives change their forms depending on their case.

➤ Note that in English, only pronouns change to reflect different functions.

    This is Peter. **He** is my friend. I gave **him** a present.

The pronouns *he* and *him* both refer to the same person, Peter. However, they change their forms to reflect their different functions in sentences, with subjects appearing as *he* and objects as *him*.

➢ The four cases in German reflect the following grammatical functions:

case	function	example		Japanese case particle
nominative	subject predicate noun	**Der Vater** singt. Er ist **Vater**.	*The father is singing.* *He is a father.*	…は・が
genitive	demonstrates possession	Das ist das Haus **des Vaters**.	*This is the house of the father.*	…の
dative	indirect object	Er dankt **dem Vater**.	*He thanks the father.*	…に
accusative	direct object	Sie liebt **den Vater**.	*She loves the father.*	…を

Note that while in English, grammatical function is marked solely by word order, in German, it is marked on nouns (*Vater*, *Vaters*) and their accompanying articles (*der*, *des*, *dem*, *den*), which change according to their function.

➢ The following table presents all case forms of nouns accompanied by a definite article. Note that the article therefore indicates the noun's case as well as its gender (and its number ⇒ Lesson 3 Grammar 2). The case forms are collectively referred to as "declensions." The genitive forms of masculine and neuter nouns add the suffix -*(e)s*.

	masculine	feminine	neuter
nominative	**der** Vater	**die** Mutter	**das** Kind
genitive	**des** Vaters	**der** Mutter	**des** Kind[e]s
dative	**dem** Vater	**der** Mutter	**dem** Kind
accusative	**den** Vater	**die** Mutter	**das** Kind

➢ The following chart demonstrates how to decline nouns preceded by an indefinite article. Both charts should be memorized in an early stage of the study process, since they are core elements of German grammar.

	masculine	feminine	neuter
nominative	**ein** Vater	**eine** Mutter	**ein** Kind
genitive	**eines** Vaters	**einer** Mutter	**eines** Kind[e]s
dative	**einem** Vater	**einer** Mutter	**einem** Kind
accusative	**einen** Vater	**eine** Mutter	**ein** Kind

Grammar 4 - Verbs: Present Tense (Irregular Verbs: *haben* and *werden*)

Sein (to be ⇒ Lesson 1 Grammar 4), *haben* (to have), and *werden* (to become) are the most important irregular verbs. They all should be memorized thoroughly, since they are also used as auxiliary verbs for more advanced structures, such as the present perfect (⇒ Lesson 10 Grammar 1) or the passive (⇒ Lesson 12 Grammar 1).

infinitive	haben (to have)		werden (to become)	
	singular	plural	singular	plural
first person	ich **habe**	wir **haben**	ich **werde**	wir **werden**
second person	du **hast**	ihr **habt**	du **wirst**	ihr **werdet**
	Sie **haben**	Sie **haben**	Sie **werden**	Sie **werden**
third person	er, sie, es **hat**	sie **haben**	er, sie, es **wird**	sie **werden**

Ich **habe** einen Fernseher. Er **wird** Polizist.
[*I have a TV set.*] [*He becomes a policeman.*]

Omission of Articles

In some cases, definite and indefinite articles are omitted, such as before nationalities, professions, proper names (of persons, towns, countries, continents [with some exceptions]), and unspecified or abstract expressions.

Ich bin Japaner. *I am Japanese.*   **Ich wohne in Berlin.** *I live in Berlin.*
Ich bin Student. *I am a student.*   **Ich habe Geld.** *I have money.*
Ich trinke Bier. *I drink beer.*   **Ich habe Fieber.** *I have a fever.*

Masculine and Feminine Forms - Professions and Nationalities

Professions and nationalities are expressed in either masculine or feminine form. Many of the feminine forms are composed of the suffix *-in* added to the masculine form.

Ich bin Student. *I am a (male) student.*
Ich bin Studentin. *I am a (female) student.*
Ich bin Japaner. *I am a (male) Japanese.*
Ich bin Japanerin. *I am a (female) Japanese.*

Deutsch auf Englisch — Lesson 2 - Directions

Exercise 1 【Grammar 1】

Use your dictionary to find out gender and meaning of the following nouns. Note the gender using the symbols *r*, *e* and *s*.

① _s_ Bein __leg__ ② ___ Blume _____ ③ ___ Fahrer _____ ④ ___ Erkältung _____ ⑤ ___ Gabel _____ ⑥ ___ Kindergarten _____ ⑦ ___ Rathaus _____ ⑧ ___ Unterricht _____ ⑨ ___ Vase _____ ⑩ ___ Zwiebel _____

Exercise 2 【Grammar 2】

Fill in the blanks with the correct forms of indefinite articles _____, definite articles _____, and personal pronouns ____.

① Da kommt _____ Frau. _____ Frau ist Lehrerin. _____ ist sehr nett. *There comes a woman* (*e* Frau). *The woman is a teacher. She is very nice.*

② Dort spielt _____ Kind. _____ Kind ist noch klein. _____ ist drei Jahre alt. *There is a child* (*s* Kind) *playing. The child is still small. It is three years old.*

③ Hier steht _____ Tisch. _____ Tisch ist aus Holz. _____ ist sehr schwer. *Here is a table* (*r* Tisch). *The table is made of wood. It is very heavy.*

Exercise 3 【Grammar 3】

Fill in the blanks with the correct forms of definite articles _____ and indefinite articles _____. For the gender of some of the nouns, refer to the vocabulary list given on page 24.

① _____ Mutter schenkt _____ Katze _____ Fisch. *The mother* (*e* Mutter) *gives a fish to the cat.*

② _____ Mädchen ist _____ Tochter _____ Mutter. *The girl* (*s* Mädchen) *is the daughter* (*e* Tochter) *of the mother.*

③ _____ Mädchen isst _____ Wurst. *The girl eats a sausage.*

④ _____ Wurst riecht gut. *The sausage smells good.*

⑤ Auf _____ Tisch steht _____ Kuchen. *On the table there is a cake.* [Hint: In this case, the preposition *auf* is followed by a dative object. (prepositions ⇒ Lesson 5 Grammar 2)]

Exercise 4 【Grammar 4】

Fill in the correct form of *haben*.

① _____ du einen Bruder? *Do you have a brother?*

② Leider _____ ich kein Geld. *Unfortunately I don't have any money.*

③ Sie _____ einen Hund. *She has a dog.*

④ Sie _____ eine Katze. *They have a cat.*

Deutsch auf Englisch — Lesson 2 - Directions

Speaking Exercise 1 🔊 13

Practice asking/giving directions with your partner. Use the map given below and ask for directions to the buildings numbered ① to ⑤.

● Entschuldigen Sie bitte, wo finde ich <u>das</u> Rathaus?   *Excuse me, where can I find the town hall?*

◇ Gehen Sie <u>hier geradeaus und dann links</u>.   *Go straight ahead and then turn left.*

● Danke schön.   *Thank you.*

[definite article, accusative]   [indefinite article, accusative]

Speaking Exercise 2 🔊 14

Now ask for directions to the buildings numbered ⑥ to ⑩.

● Entschuldigung, ich suche <u>**einen** Supermarkt</u>...   *Excuse me, I am looking for a supermarket...*

◇ Gehen Sie <u>gleich hier rechts</u>. Auf der <u>rechten</u> Seite ist <u>ein Supermarkt</u>.   *Just turn right here. On the right hand side there is a supermarket.*

● Vielen Dank.   *Thank you.*

① *s* **Rathaus** town hall   ② *r* **Bahnhof** station   ③ *r* **Park** park   ④ *e* **Universität** university   ⑤ *e* **Post** post office   ⑥ *r* **Supermarkt** supermarket   ⑦ *e* **Bank** bank   ⑧ *e* **Apotheke** chemist's shop   ⑨ *s* **Café** café   ⑩ *r* **Parkplatz** car park

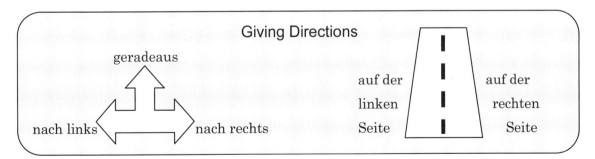

23 - dreiundzwanzig

Deutsch auf Englisch

Lesson 2 - Directions

Objectives

In this lesson you have learned how to
- ✓ communicate with passers-by/strangers
- ✓ ask for directions
- ✓ give directions

Vocabulary - Basic Nouns 1 🔊 15

1 *r* Topf, ¨e *pot*
2 *r* Besen, - *broom*
3 *r* Tisch, -e *table*
4 *r* Stuhl, ¨e *chair*
5 *r* Kühlschrank, ¨e *refrigerator*
6 *r* Fisch, -e *fish*
7 *e* Wurst, ¨e *sausage*
8 *r* Kuchen, - *cake*

9 *e* Katze, -n *cat*
10 *r* Teller, - *plate*
11 *s* Messer, - *knife*
12 *e* Pfanne, -n *frying pan*
13 *s* Glas, ¨er *glas*
14 *r* Herd, -e *stove*
15 *s* Handtuch, ¨er *towel*

Lesson 3 - Shopping

Dialogue - Eine Ansichtskarte kostet zwei Euro. 🔊 16

- Entschuldigen Sie bitte, wo haben Sie denn Ansichtskarten?
- ◇ Ansichtskarten sind dort drüben.
- Danke. Was kosten denn die hier?
- ◇ Eine Ansichtskarte kostet zwei Euro.
- Gut, dann nehme ich drei Stück.
- ◇ Hier, bitte sehr. Das macht sechs Euro.

e Ansichtskarte, -n	*picture postcard*
dort drüben	*over there*
kosten	*to cost*
r Euro	*euro € (1 € = 100 cent)*
dann	*then, well, in this case*
nehmen	*to take, to have*
s Stück	*piece, article*
bitte sehr	*here you are*
Das macht ...	*That is/That comes to ...*

Asking for Prices - *How much is ...?* 🔊 17

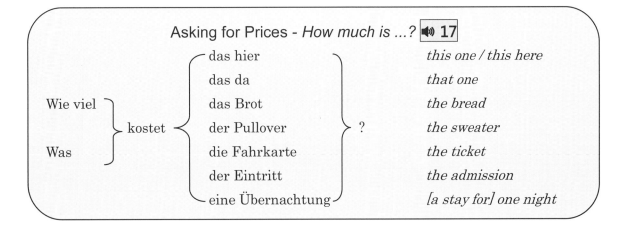

Grammar 1 - Noun Plurals

➢ Although a few German nouns form their plurals by adding an -*s* to the singular in the same way most English nouns do, German plurals are more complex than their English counterparts. First, the plural forms of German nouns can be grouped into the following five patterns according to the type of ending added to the singular noun.

	singular	plural	English translation
singular noun + (no ending)	der Lehrer	die Lehrer	*teacher*
	die Mutter	die Mütter	*mother*
singular noun + -e	der Tag	die Tage	*day*
	der Arzt	die Ärzte	*physician*
singular noun + -er	das Buch	die Bücher	*book*
singular noun + -(e)n	die Schwester	die Schwestern	*sister*
	die Frau	die Frauen	*woman*
singular noun + -s	das Auto	die Autos	*car*

➢ Note the spelling changes of a stem vowel (*a*, *o*, *u*, or *au*) into an umlaut form, which generally occur if there is no ending or if the ending -*er* is added; this also sometimes takes place when adding -*e*.

➢ All plural forms (in the nominative) take *die* as the definite article, regardless of gender. Be careful not to confuse plurals preceded by *die* with feminine singular nouns. To tell them apart, it is advisable to memorize the possible plural endings. A noun preceded by *die* is especially likely to be plural if it ends in -*e*, -*er*, -*(e)n*, or -*s*.

➢ Like the English indefinite articles *a* and *an*, the German indefinite article *ein* has no plural form.

    Das ist ein Auto.   *This is a car.*
    Das sind ☐ Autos.   *These are ☐ cars.*

➢ Although a rather complicated system of rules exists that govern the patterns of plural formation to be used with certain nouns (e.g., plurals of loanwords are generally formed by adding -*s*; feminine nouns often take -*(e)n* to form their plural), beginners should memorize nouns together with their plural forms (and their genders ⇒ Lesson 2 Grammar 1).

- The plural form of a noun can be found in a dictionary. Since dictionaries also show the endings for genitive singular forms, make sure not to mistake these endings for the plurals.

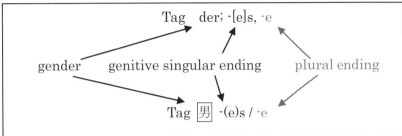

- When referring to a plural noun, the personal pronoun *sie* (not to be confused with the third-person feminine singular *sie* [*she*]) is used.

  <u>Die Bücher</u> sind teuer.   <u>*The books*</u> *are expensive.*

  Sie sind sehr interessant.   ***They*** *are very interesting.*

Grammar 2 - Declension of Plural Nouns

- Like singular nouns, plural nouns also take one of the four cases (nominative, genitive, dative, or accusative).

singular nominative		der Bruder [*the brother*]	die Schwester [*the sister*]	das Hotel [*the hotel*]
plural	nominative	**die Brüder**	**die Schwestern**	**die Hotels**
	genitive	**der** Brüder	**der** Schwestern	**der** Hotels
	dative	**den Brüdern**	**den** Schwestern	**den** Hotels
	accusative	**die** Brüder	**die** Schwestern	**die** Hotels

- Note that all plural forms take the same article per case, regardless of their gender.
- In the dative plural, the ending *-n* is added to the noun, unless the plural form already ends in *-n* or *-s*.

Grammar 3 - Declension of Weak Nouns

	singular	plural
nominative	der Student [*the student*]	die Student**en**
genitive	des Student**en**	der Student**en**
dative	dem Student**en**	den Student**en**
accusative	den Student**en**	die Student**en**

➤ Some masculine (and in a few cases neuter) nouns take the ending *-en* in all cases except the nominative singular. These nouns are referred to as "weak nouns," and in most cases, they denote living beings. Here are some examples:

der Junge [*boy*], der Mensch [*human*], der Tourist [*tourist*], der Polizist [*policeman*]

➤ Since weak nouns in the singular are easy to confuse with their plural forms, close attention must be paid to their articles, and contexts. The dative plural and accusative singular have identical articles and endings.

Der Professor schenkt <u>den Studenten</u> Bücher.	*The professor presents <u>the students</u> with books.* [dative plural]
Der Professor mag <u>den Studenten</u>.	*The professor likes <u>the student</u>.* [accusative singular]
Der Professor mag <u>die Studenten</u>.	*The professor likes <u>the students</u>.* [accusative plural]

Grammar 4 - The Numbers 0-100

➤ Numerals from *dreizehn* [thirteen] to *neunzehn* [nineteen] are constructed similarly to those of English, but they include some irregular forms (***sech**zehn* [sixteen], ***sieb**zehn* [seventeen]).

➤ Numerals from *zwanzig* [twenty] onwards, however, are read from the second digit to the first digit, with *und* [and] added between.

3̄5   thirtȳfive   fünf**und**dreißig

➤ Numbers are feminine.

Der Torwart hat die Eins.   *The goal keeper has the player number 1.*

➤ For cardinal numbers from 100 to 1,000,000 refer to ⇒ Lesson 6 Grammar 4; for ordinal numbers, refer to ⇒ Supplement 5.

Deutsch auf Englisch   Lesson 3 - Shopping

Exercise 1 【Grammar 1】

Use a dictionary to find out the plural forms of the following nouns and arrange them accordingly: *Lehrer, Schüler, Brief, Kleid, Frau, Kind, Mutter, Rose, Baby, Windel*.

singular noun + (no ending)   der Lehrer – die Lehrer   _____ - _____   _____ - _____
singular noun + -*e*   _____ - _____
singular noun + -*er*   _____ - _____   _____ - _____
singular noun + -(*e*)*n*   _____ - _____   _____ - _____   _____ - _____
singular noun + -*s*   _____ - _____

Exercise 2 【Grammar 2】

Rewrite the given sentences by changing the underlined nouns into their plural forms (⇒ Exercise 1). If necessary, also adjust the form of the verb.

① Der Lehrer schreibt dem Schüler einen Brief. *The teacher writes the pupil a letter.*
→_____

② Das Kleid der Frau ist schön. *The woman's dress is nice.*
→_____

③ Zum Muttertag kauft das Kind der Mutter eine Rose. *On Mother's Day, the child buys a rose for the mother.*
→_____

④ Ein Baby braucht eine Windel. *A baby needs a diaper.*
→_____

Exercise 3 【Grammar 3】

Orally practice the declension (singular and plural) of the following weak nouns.

① *r* Kunde, -n *customer* ← der Kunde, des Kunden, dem Kunden, …
② *r* Biologe, -n *biologist*
③ *r* Philosoph, -en *philosopher*
④ *r* Affe, -n *monkey*

Exercise 4 【Grammar 4】

Read the numbers from 0 to 100 two times aloud (⇒ Basics 3). Then write down the numbers given below following the example.

(ex) zweiunddreißig   32   ③ achtundneunzig   _____
① fünfundsechzig   _____   ④ siebenundfünfzig   _____
② neununddreißig   _____   ⑤ siebzehn   _____

Deutsch auf Englisch   **Lesson 3 - Shopping**

Speaking Exercise 1 【Grammar 1,4】 🔊 18

Practice shopping at the kiosk with your partner using the sentences below. Swap the underlined words with those given in the vocabulary on ⇒ page 31.

◇ Guten Tag, haben Sie Bleistifte?　　　*Hello. Do you sell pencils?*
● Ja, Bleistifte sind gleich hier. Ein　　*Yes, pencils are right here. One pencil*
　Bleistift kostet ein Euro fünfzig Cent.　*costs one euro fifty cent.*
◇ Dann nehme ich zwei Bleistifte.　　　*Then I take two pencils.*
● Vielen Dank. Das macht drei Euro.　　*Thank you. That is three euros please.*

Speaking Exercise 2 【Grammar 4】 🔊 19

Talk with your partner about the age (*Alter*), telephone number (*Telefonnummer*), and number of siblings (*Geschwister*) of the persons depicted below by changing the underlined parts. Finally, ask each other about your age, telephone number, and number of siblings.

> **seine** *his*, **ihre** *her*, **deine** *your*, **meine** *my* (possessive adjectives ⇒ Lesson 6 Grammar 2)

◇ Wie alt ist Maria?　　　　　　　　*How old is Maria?*
● Sie ist neunzehn Jahre alt.　　　　　*She is nineteen years old.*
◇ Wie ist ihre Telefonnummer?　　　　*What is her telephone number?*
●　　Ihre　Telefonnummer　ist　　*Her telephone number is 065-4322-5351.*
　065-4322-5351. ◀ ── null-sechs-fünf-vier-...
◇ Wie viele Geschwister hat sie?　　　*How many siblings does she have?*
● Sie hat drei Geschwister.　　　　　　*She has three siblings.*

	Maria	Herr Fischer	Christian	ich	mein/e Partner/in
Alter	19	54	25		
Telefon-nummer	065-4322-5351	0171-342-564	030-3536-3423		
Geschwister	3	0	2		

Note: If there are no siblings: *Ich habe keine Geschwister.* (*keine* = negative indefinite article ⇒ Lesson 6 Grammar 2,3). In case there is one brother or sister: *Ich habe einen Bruder. / Ich habe eine Schwester.*

Deutsch auf Englisch　　　　　　　　　　　**Lesson 3 - Shopping**

Objectives

In this lesson you have learned how to
- ✓ ask for prices of goods
- ✓ purchase goods
- ✓ ask for telephone numbers / the age of persons
- ✓ count from 0 to 100

Vocabulary - Basic Nouns 2 🔊 20

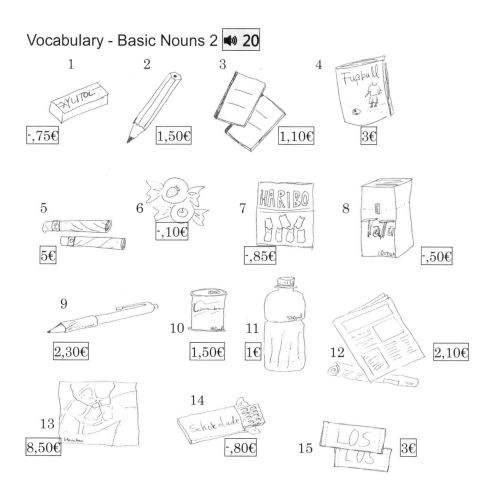

1 *r* Kaugummi, -s *chewing gum*
2 *r* Bleistift, -e *pencil*
3 *s* Notizbuch, ¨-er *notebook*
4 *e* Zeitschrift, -en *magazine*
5 *e* Zigarre, -n *cigar*
6 *s* Bonbon, -s *candy*
7 *e* Tüte, -n Gummibärchen *bag of jelly babies*
8 *e* Packung, -en Taschentücher *pack of handkerchieves*
9 *r* Kugelschreiber, - *ball pen*
10 *e* Dose, -n Bier *can of beer*
11 *e* Flasche, -n Wasser *bottle of water*
12 *e* Zeitung, -en *newspaper*
13 *r* Stadtplan, ¨-e *city map*
14 *e* Schokolade, -n *chocolate*
15 *s* Los, -e *lottery ticket*

Lesson 4 - Hobbies and Preferences

Dialogue - Was ist eigentlich dein Hobby?
🔊 21

- ● Was ist eigentlich dein Hobby?
- ◇ Ich spiele gern Tennis. Und du? Was machst du denn in der Freizeit?
- ● Ich mache nicht so gern Sport. Ich lese lieber. Am liebsten lese ich Mangas. Liest du auch gern?
- ◇ Nein, gar nicht. Aber ich sehe oft Fernsehserien und gehe manchmal ins Kino. Gehst du nicht auch gern ins Kino?
- ● Doch, das macht mir auch Spaß!

eigentlich (here:) *by the way*
s **Hobby, -s** *hobby*
gern *like*
machen *to do*
e **Freizeit, -en** *spare time*
nicht so gern *do not like so much*
lieber *prefer* (comparative of *gern* ⇒ Lesson 11 Grammar 2)
am liebsten *like best* (superlative of *gern* ⇒ Lesson 11 Grammar 2)
gar nicht *not at all*
aber *but*
manchmal *sometimes*
doch *yes* (⇒ "How to Use *ja, nein, doch*" below)
Spaß machen *find something fun*
→ for further vocabulary see ⇒ Speaking Exercise, page 37)

How to Use *ja, nein, doch* 🔊 22

Spielst du gern Fußball?
Do you like playing soccer?
- ⊕ Ja, ich spiele gern Fußball. *Yes, I do.*
- ⊖ Nein, ich spiele nicht gern Fußball. *No, I don't.*

Spielst du <u>nicht</u> gern Fußball?
Don't you like playing soccer?
- ⊕ **Doch**, ich spiele gern Fußball.
  *Yes, I do. / **Actually** I do. / **On the contrary**, I do.*
- ⊖ Nein, ich spiele nicht gern Fußball.
  No, I don't.

When answering a negative question positively in German, *doch* is used instead of *ja*.

Grammar 1 - Verbs: Present Tense (Irregular Verbs)

- While the majority of German verbs, the so-called regular verbs, change their forms as explained in ⇒ Lesson 1 Grammar 2, some verbs are conjugated irregularly. In addition to adding the same endings to their stems as the regular verbs, these verbs also change their stem vowels in the second and third person singular. For example, the stem vowel *a* of the infinitive *fahren* (to drive, to travel) is changed to the umlaut form *ä* in *du fährst* (you drive) and *er/sie/es fährt* (he/she/it drives). These verbs are therefore also referred to as "stem-changing verbs."
- There are three patterns for stem-changing verbs, as shown in the table below. Furthermore, some special types of irregular verbs do not fit into theses three patterns.

	a→ä type	e→i type	e→ie type	special type
infinitive	fahren	sprechen	sehen	wissen
[translation]	[*to drive*]	[*to speak*]	[*to see*]	[*to know*]
ich	fahre	spreche	sehe	**weiß**
du	**fährst**	**sprichst**	**siehst**	**weißt**
Sie	fahren	sprechen	sehen	wissen
er / sie / es	**fährt**	**spricht**	**sieht**	**weiß**
wir	fahren	sprechen	sehen	wissen
ihr	fahrt	sprecht	seht	wisst
Sie	fahren	sprechen	sehen	wissen
sie	fahren	sprechen	sehen	wissen

- Since stem vowel changes in irregular verbs cannot be predicted, you must refer to the list of irregular verbs (⇒ Appendix I) or to your dictionary. When learning new irregular verbs, make sure to memorize them together with their respective patterns of vowel change.

Grammar 2 - Imperative

- The imperative verb form is used to give orders or commands or to formulate requests or demands. As in English, the form of the verb is determined by who and how many people are being addressed. While English distinguishes between commands given to one or more persons using the dictionary form of the verb (*Come in!*), and orders including oneself and others using *let's* and the dictionary form of the main verb (*Let's wait*), there are three types of imperatives in German: the *du* form, *ihr* form, and *Sie* form of imperatives.

➤ The *du* form is used to give an order to a single person you would address with *du*. It is formed by using the stem of the verb and, in some cases, adding the ending *-e*.
➤ The *ihr* form is used to give an order to two or more persons whom you address with *du*. It is formed by adding a *-t* to the stem of the verb.
➤ The *Sie* form is used to give an order to a single person or more persons you would address with *Sie*. It is formed by using the infinitive form of the verb, followed by *Sie*.
➤ The imperative of *sein* is constructed irregularly, as shown in the chart below. Also, e→i/ie-type irregular verbs change their stem vowels in the *du* form imperative.

geben [*to give*; e→i type]   →   du gibst   →   Gib! *Give!*

	basic type	e→i/ie type	special type
infinitive	kommen [*to come*]	sprechen [*to speak*]	sein [*to be*]
du form imperative	Komm(e)!	Sprich!	**Sei!**
ihr form imperative	Kommt!	Sprecht!	**Seid!**
Sie form imperative	Kommen Sie!	Sprechen Sie!	**Seien** Sie!

➤ Note that as in English, imperative subjects in German are omitted in the *du* and *ihr* forms. However, the German *Sie* form requires the subject *Sie*.
➤ Unlike imperative sentences in English, imperative sentences in German normally end with an exclamation mark.

Warte hier**!**   *Wait here.*

➤ As in English, a command or request using an imperative verb form can be softened by including a friendly *bitte* (please).

Geben Sie mir das Salz!   *Give me the salt.*
Geben Sie mir **bitte** das Salz!   ***Please*** *give me the salt.*

Grammar 3 - Personal Pronouns (Dative, Accusative)

➤ Like English pronouns, German personal pronouns are used as not only subjects (⇒ Lesson 1 Grammar 1) but also as direct or indirect objects. However, while the English language uses only one objective case for pronouns, German distinguishes between dative and accusative pronouns as shown in the example and chart below.

Sie ist meine Freundin.   ***She*** *is my girlfriend.* [*sie* = personal pronoun nominative]
Ich liebe **sie**.   *I love **her**.* [*sie* = personal pronoun accusative]
Ich schenke **ihr** einen Ring.   *I give **her** a ring.* [*ihr* = personal pronoun dative]

		first person	second person		third person		
singular	dative	mir	dir	Ihnen	ihm	ihr	ihm
	accusative	mich	dich	Sie	ihn	sie	es
	English objective pronoun	me	you		him	her	it
plural	dative	uns	euch	Ihnen	ihnen		
	accusative	uns	euch	Sie	sie		
	English objective pronoun	us	you		them		

➤ Similar to nominative pronouns, the English objective pronoun *you* corresponds to multiple German pronouns, both dative and accusative, singular and plural (⇒ Lesson 1 Grammar 1).

➤ Be aware that the English objective pronoun *it* also has multiple equivalents in German. As with the nominative third-person pronouns (⇒ Lesson 2 Grammar 2), *it* must be translated according to the grammatical gender of its antecedent, that is, as either *ihm*, *ihn*, *ihr*, *sie*, *ihm*, or *es*.

    Isst du den Kuchen?   *Are you going to eat the cake?* [r Kuchen *cake*]
    Ja, ich esse **ihn**.   *Yes, I am going to eat* ***it***.
    ✗ Ja, ich esse **es**.   [*ihn* = accusative pronoun, masculine]

➤ In sentences using both a dative and an accusative object in the form of pronouns, the accusative pronoun comes before the dative pronoun.

    Ich schreibe <u>meiner Mutter</u> <u>einen Brief</u>. *I write a letter to my mother.*
    Ich schreibe **<u>ihr</u>** <u>einen Brief</u>. *I write her a letter.* [*ihr* = dative pronoun]
    Ich schreibe **<u>ihn</u>** **<u>ihr</u>**. *I write it to her.* [*ihn* = accusative pronoun]

Exercise 1 【Grammar 1】

Look up the irregular verbs given in ( ) in your dictionary, the List of Common Irregular Verbs (⇒ Appendix I), or in the vocabulary on ⇒ page 38. Fill in the correct forms of the verbs and complete the sentences.

① Die Mutter _____ das Baby. (tragen) *The mother is carrying the baby.*

② Petra _____ den Ball und Thomas _____ ihn. (werfen, fangen) *Petra throws the ball and Thomas catches it.*

③ Der Hund _____ ein bisschen und _____ dann. (fressen, schlafen) *The dog eats a little bit and then sleeps.*

④ Sie _____ den Apfel, bevor sie ihn _____. (waschen, essen) *She washes the apple before eating it.*

Exercise 2 【Grammar 2】

Complete the following sentences by filling in the correct imperative forms of the verbs in ( ).

① Do your homework! (machen: →ihr)
_____ die Hausaufgaben!

② Go to school! (gehen: →du)
_____ zur Schule!

③ Do not smoke so much! (rauchen: →Sie)
_____ nicht so viel!

④ Be quiet! (sein: →ihr)
_____ still!

Exercise 3 【Grammar 3】

Rewrite the sentences by exchanging the underlined parts with personal pronouns in the correct case.

① <u>Markus</u> liebt <u>Gisela</u>. *Markus loves Gisela.*
→ _____

② <u>Der Mann</u> kauft <u>zwei Bücher</u>. *The man buys two books.*
→ _____

③ Ist das Peter's Auto? - Nein, <u>das Auto</u> gehört nicht <u>Peter</u>, sondern <u>Yvonne</u>. *Is this Peter's car? - No, this car is not Peter's but Yvonne's.*
→ _____

④ <u>Martin</u> schenkt <u>dem Mädchen</u> <u>eine Blume</u>. *Martin gives a flower to the girl.*
→ _____

Deutsch auf Englisch   Lesson 4 - Hobbies and Preferences

Speaking Exercise 【Grammar 1】 🔊 23

Exchange the underlined parts of the following example conversation with the activities depicted below. Pay attention to the correct forms of the irregular verbs. When finished, talk about your own hobbies and preferences.

be careful: change of stem vowel [*lesen* → *du liest*]

◇ <u>Liest</u> du gern <u>Romane</u>? *Do you like reading novels?*
● Nein, ich <u>lese</u> nicht so gern <u>Romane</u>. *No, I don't like reading novels that much.*
Ich <u>lese</u> lieber <u>Mangas</u>. *I prefer reading Japanese comics.*

example	①	②	③	④	⑤

spielen
to play (sports, music instruments)
Fußball *soccer*
Tennis *tennis*
Golf *golf*
Klavier *piano*
Gitarre *guitar*

lesen [e→ie]
to read
Romane *novels*
Mangas *Japanese comics*
Zeitschriften *magazines*
Gedichte *poems*
Märchen *fairy tales*

fahren [a→ä]
to drive, to ride
Auto *car*
Motorrad *motorcycle*
Fahrrad *bicycle*
Ski *ski*
Snowboard *snowboard*

sehen [e→ie]
to watch
Fußballspiele *football matches*
Filme *movies*
Fernsehserien *television series*

hören
to listen to
klassische Musik *classical music*
Pop *pop music*
Jazz *jazz music*
Schlager *hit songs*

essen [e→i]
to eat
Schokolade *chocolate*
Pizza *pizza*
Gemüse *vegetables*
Fisch *fish*
Fleisch *meat*

Deutsch auf Englisch — Lesson 4 - Hobbies and Preferences

Objectives

In this lesson you have learned how to

✓ ask and give information about hobbies and preferences

✓ request somebody to do something

✓ answer correctly to yes-no-questions

Vocabulary - Irregular Verbs 🔊 24

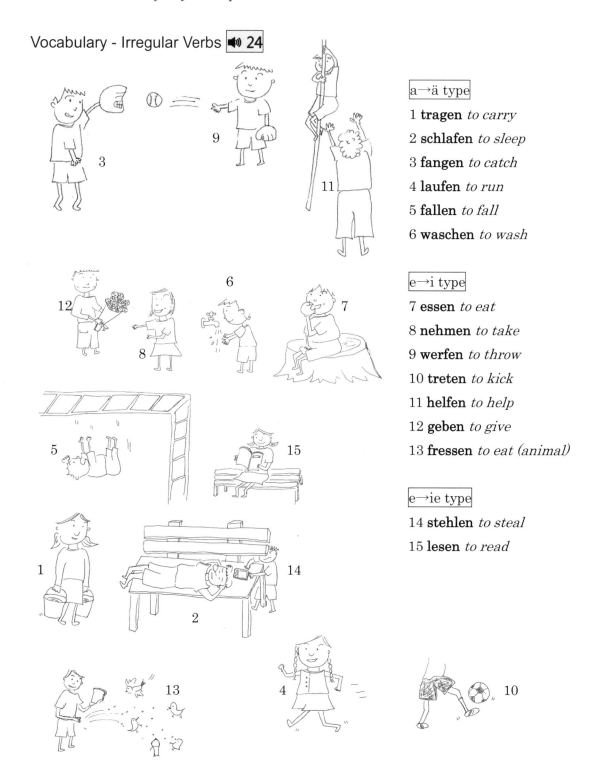

a→ä type

1 **tragen** *to carry*
2 **schlafen** *to sleep*
3 **fangen** *to catch*
4 **laufen** *to run*
5 **fallen** *to fall*
6 **waschen** *to wash*

e→i type

7 **essen** *to eat*
8 **nehmen** *to take*
9 **werfen** *to throw*
10 **treten** *to kick*
11 **helfen** *to help*
12 **geben** *to give*
13 **fressen** *to eat (animal)*

e→ie type

14 **stehlen** *to steal*
15 **lesen** *to read*

Lesson 5 - Transportation

Dialogue - Wo bekomme ich eine Fahrkarte? 🔊 25

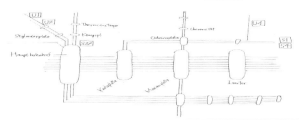

- Entschuldigen Sie, welche S-Bahn fährt zum Hauptbahnhof?
- ◇ Die Linie 8.
- Und wo bekomme ich eine Fahrkarte für die S-Bahn?
- ◇ Da vorne, am Automaten oder am Kiosk. Ich glaube, die nächste S-Bahn fährt um 9:15 Uhr.
- Und wie spät ist es jetzt?
- ◇ Schon 9:12 Uhr. Beeilen Sie sich!
- Danke!

welche **welch** *which* (*der* words ⇒ Lesson 6 Grammar 1)
e S-Bahn, -en *city railway*
r Hauptbahnhof *main station*
e Linie, -n *line, number*
bekommen *to be able to get / buy*
e Fahrkarte, -n *ticket*
r Automat, -en *ticket machine*
nächste **nächst** *next*
sich beeilen *to hurry up* (reflexive verb ⇒ Lesson 8 Grammar 3)

Expressions of Time 🔊 26

Wie spät ist es jetzt? / Wie viel Uhr ist es jetzt? *What time is it?*

[formal - radio / station / timetables / ...] / [informal - everyday language]

17:00 Uhr	Es ist siebzehn Uhr. / Es ist fünf.
17:10 Uhr	Es ist siebzehn Uhr zehn. / Es ist zehn nach fünf.
17:15 Uhr	Es ist siebzehn Uhr fünfzehn. / Es ist Viertel nach fünf. *(quarter past)*
17:25 Uhr	Es ist siebzehn Uhr fünfundzwanzig. / Es ist fünf vor halb **sechs**.
17:30 Uhr	Es ist siebzehn Uhr dreißig. / Es ist halb sechs. ← *half past five*
17:45 Uhr	Es ist siebzehn Uhr fünfundvierzig. / Es ist Viertel vor sechs. *(quarter to)*
17:55 Uhr	Es ist siebzehn Uhr fünfundfünfzig. / Es ist fünf vor sechs.

Wann? / Um wie viel Uhr? *When? At what time?*

→ **um** siebzehn Uhr *at five o'clock*   **gegen** siebzehn Uhr *around five o'clock*

Grammar 1 - Prepositions I (Prepositions Taking the Genitive, Dative, or Accusative)

- Like English prepositions, German prepositions are placed in front of nouns or pronouns to indicate the relationship between these nouns or pronouns and other parts of the sentence relating to time, manner, location, or direction.

    Ich lebe **in** New York.   *I live **in** New York.* [preposition indicating location]

    Wir fahren **ohne** Peter.   *We go **without** Peter.* [preposition indicating manner]

- However, English nouns or pronouns preceded by prepositions do not change their forms. German nouns or pronouns take genitive, dative, or accusative forms following prepositions, depending on the preposition.

    Der Mann geht **durch** den Park. *The man goes through the park.* [**durch** = accusative preposition]

    Der Mann kommt **aus** dem Park. *The man comes out of the park.* [**aus** = dative preposition]

- German prepositions are therefore grouped into the following categories. (A fourth category, so called "two-way prepositions" are explained in ⇒ Grammar 2.)

A genitive prepositions		
main prepositions	**(an)statt** *instead of* **trotz** *despite* **während** *during* **wegen** *because of*	
examples	**während** des Krieges *during the war*, **wegen** der Krankheit *because of the illness*	
B dative prepositions		
main prepositions	**aus** *from, out* **bei** *at, by* **mit** *with, by* **nach** *after* **seit** *since* **von** *from, by, of* **zu** *to, for*	
examples	**aus** dem Zimmer *out of the room*, **mit** dir *with you*, **zu** den Eltern *to the parents*	
C accusative prepositions		
main prepositions	**durch** *through* **für** *for* **ohne** *without* **um** *around, at, about* **gegen** *against*	
examples	**durch** das Fenster *through the window*, **für** den Frieden *for the peace*, **um** zwei Uhr *at two o'clock*	

- When learning prepositions, it is crucial to also memorize the cases they take, that is, to which of the above groups each belongs.

- Likewise, when learning a new verb, the preposition(s) accompanying them should also be memorized, since the prepositions following the verb often exert considerable influence on the meaning of the verb.

    Ich **komme aus** Berlin. *I come from Berlin.*

    Ich **komme um** meinen Lohn. *I miss out on my reward.*

    Ich **komme auf** einen guten Plan. *I think of a good plan.*

Grammar 2 - Prepositions II (Two-Way Prepositions)

➤ So-called two-way prepositions are either followed by the dative or the accusative, depending on the verb with which they appear.

➤ If the verb denotes a location (*Wo?* (*Where?*)), the preposition is followed by a dative object; if the verb indicates a motion in a particular direction (*Wohin?* (*Where to?*)), an accusative object follows it.

Wo arbeiten Sie? *Where do you work?*

Ich arbeite **in der Innenstadt**. *I work in the town center.* [location→dative]

Wohin fahren Sie? *Where do you go to?*

Ich fahre **in die Innenstadt**. *I go to the town center.* [direction→accusative]

➤ There are nine two-way prepositions in German, as shown in the chart below.

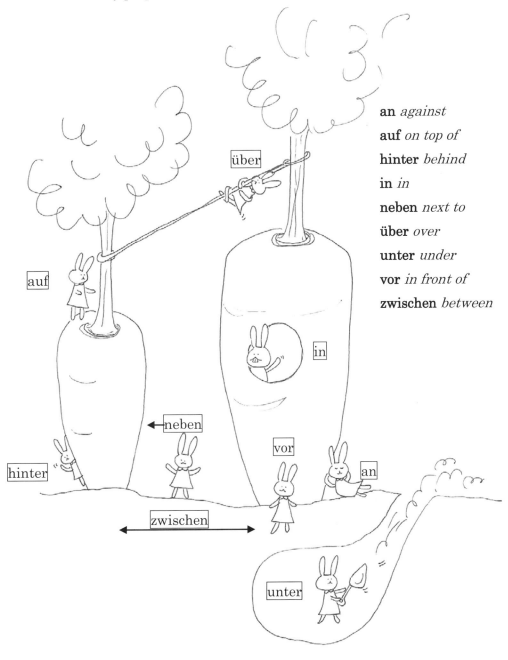

an *against*
auf *on top of*
hinter *behind*
in *in*
neben *next to*
über *over*
unter *under*
vor *in front of*
zwischen *between*

Grammar 3 - Contraction of Prepositions and Definite Articles

➤ If the definite articles *der*, *das*, or *dem* following a preposition are not stressed, they are often contracted with the preposition. These contracted forms are commonly used in both spoken and written German. Examples of some common contractions include the following:

am (an dem) → **am** Abend *in the evening*
im (in dem) → **im** Winter *in the winter*
ins (in das) → **ins** Theater *to the theater*
vom (von dem) → **vom** Rathaus *from the town hall*
zum (zu dem) → **zum** Geburtstag *for one's birthday*
zur (zu der) → **zur** Schule *to school*

Grammar 4 - *Da*-Compounds

➤ If the object of a preposition refers to an inanimate object (a thing or an idea), it can be replaced by a combination of *da* and the preposition (or *dar* + preposition if the preposition begins with a vowel).

Fährst du mit dem Auto nach Dresden? *Do you go to Dresden in this car?*
- Ja, ich fahre **damit**. *Yes, I use it.*   **damit** = mit dem Auto
Liegt das Buch auf dem Tisch? *Is the book on the table?*
- Ja, es liegt **darauf**. *Yes, it is on it.*   **darauf** = auf dem Tisch

➤ If the object of a preposition refers to a person or an animal, a prepositional phrase or an object pronoun must be used instead.

Fährst du mit dem Professor nach Dresden? *Do you go to Dresden with the professor?*
- Ja, ich fahre **mit ihm**. *Yes, I go **with him**.*
× Ja, ich fahre ~~damit~~.

German Proverbs – deutsche Sprichwörter (3)

Wo ein Wille ist, ist auch ein Weg.

Where there is a will, there is a way.

Deutsch auf Englisch — Lesson 5 - Transportation

Exercise 1 【Grammar 1,3】

Fill in the correct prepositions (....), definite articles (____), and contractions of prepositions and articles (____).

① _____ _____ Fahrrades bekomme ich Geld _____ Geburtstag. *For my birthday* (*r* Geburtstag), *I get money instead of the bicycle* (*s* Fahrrad).

② Heute gehe ich _____ _____ Park _____ Schule. *Today I go through the park* (*r* Park) *to school* (*e* Schule).

③ _____ _____ Regens fahre ich _____ _____ Taxi. *Because of the rain* (*r* Regen), *I go by taxi* (*s* Taxi).

④ _____ Winter gehen wir oft _____ Hallenbad. *In the winter* (*r* Winter), *we often go to the indoor pool* (*s* Hallenbad).

⑤ Er arbeitet _____ _____ Zweiten Weltkrieg _____ _____ Post. *He has been working at the post office* (*e* Post) *since World War II* (*r* Zweite Weltkrieg).

Exercise 2 【Grammar 2】

Complete the following sentences using definite articles in the appropriate case.

① Erna setzt die Katze vor _____ Ofen. *Erna puts the cat in front of the stove* (*r* Ofen).

② Ich hänge das Bild an _____ Wand über _____ Schreibtisch. *I put the painting on the wall* (*e* Wand) *above the desk* (*r* Schreibtisch).

③ Die Uhr hängt an _____ Wand über _____ Fernseher. *The clock is on the wall above the TV* (*r* Fernseher).

④ Der Hund sitzt unter _____ Tisch. *The dog is sitting under the table* (*r* Tisch).

⑤ Das Mädchen springt über _____ Pfütze. *The girl is jumping over the puddle* (*e* Pfütze).

Exercise 3 【Grammar 4】

Rewrite the sentences, exchanging the underlined prepositional phrase with the correct *da*-compound.

① Ich sitze auf dem Stuhl. *I sit on the chair.*
   → _____

② Martina spielt mit dem Ball. *Martina plays with the ball.*
   → _____

③ Wir sprechen über den Roman. *We talk about the novel.*
   → _____

④ Das kommt von der Angst. *That is due to the anxiety.*
   → _____

Deutsch auf Englisch — Lesson 5 - Transportation

Speaking Exercise 1 【Grammar 1】 🔊 27

Talk with your partner about your means of transport and the time it takes to get to university every day. For the necessary vocabulary refer to ⇒ page 45. Note that the means of transportation is expressed by using the preposition *mit*, except for *zu Fuß* [walking]).

◇ Womit kommst du zur Universität? *How do you come to university?*
● Ich komme mit dem Fahrrad. *I come by bicycle.*
◇ Wie lange brauchst du? *How long does it take you?*
● Ich brauche etwa eine halbe Stunde. *It takes me about half an hour.*

Talking about duration

Wie lange? *How long?*

○○Minuten ○○ *minutes*
eine Stunde *one hour*
○○Stunden ○○ *hours*
eine Viertelstunde *a quarter of an hour*
eine halbe Stunde *half an hour*
eine Dreiviertelstunde *three-quarters of an hour*
dreieinhalb Stunden *three and a half hours*

Speaking Exercise 2 【Grammar 1,2,3】 🔊 28

Talk with your partner about your travel plans for the next holidays.

◇ Wohin fährst du in den Ferien? *Where will you go during the holidays?*
● Ich fahre nach Berlin. *I will go to Berlin.*

countries, places, etc. → nach+dative		nach Japan *to Japan*, nach England *to England*, nach München *to Munich*
persons → zu+dative		zu meinen Eltern *to my parents*, zu meiner Freundin *to my girlfriend*, zu meinen Verwandten *to my relatives* [⇒ Lesson 6 Grammar 2]
mountains, forests, etc. → in+accusative		in die Berge *into the mountains*, in den Westerwald *to the Westerwald* [region in middle Germany], in die Alpen *into the alps*
islands, etc. → auf+accusative		auf die Insel Borkum *to the island of Borkum*
lakes, oceans, rivers, etc. → an+accusative		an den Rhein *to the river Rhein*, ans Meer *to the seaside*, an den See *to the lake*

Deutsch auf Englisch — Lesson 5 - Transportation

Objectives

In this lesson you have learned how to
- ✓ express and ask for the time and duration
- ✓ ask questions concerning transportation
- ✓ talk about means of transportation and destinations

Vocabulary - Basic Nouns 3 🔊 29

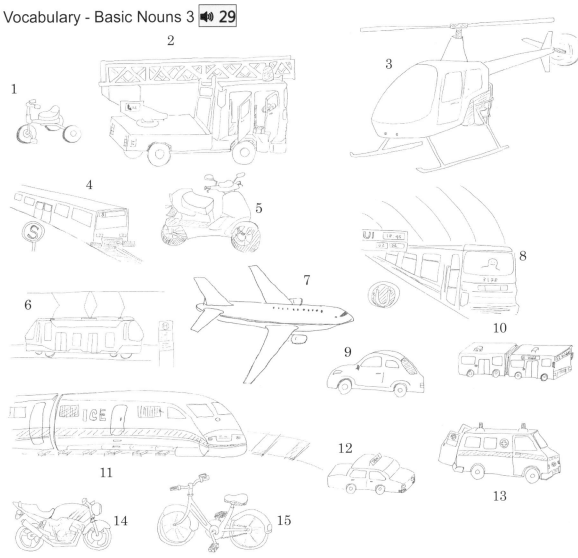

1 *s* Dreirad, ¨-er *tricycle*
2 *s* Feuerwehrauto, -s *fire engine*
3 *r* Hubschrauber, - *helicopter*
4 *e* S-Bahn, -en *city railway*
5 *r* Motorroller, - *motor scooter*
6 *e* Straßenbahn, -en *tram*
7 *s* Flugzeug, -e *airplane*
8 *e* U-Bahn, -en *subway*
9 *s* Auto, -s *car*
10 *r* Bus, Busse *bus*
11 *r* Zug, ¨-e *train*
12 *s* Taxi, -s *taxi*
13 *r* Krankenwagen, - *ambulance*
14 *s* Motorrad, ¨-er *motorcycle*
15 *s* Fahrrad, ¨-er *bicycle*

Lesson 6 - Invitations

Dialogue - Dazu habe ich keine Lust. 🔊 30

- ● Hallo Manfred, lange nicht gesehen! Wie geht es dir?
- ◇ Nicht so gut.
- ● Komm, gehen wir zusammen italienisch essen!
- ◇ Nein, dazu habe ich keine Lust. Ich mag keine Spaghetti und auch keine Pizza. Ich esse nie italienisch.
- ● Gehen wir dann einen Kaffee trinken?
- ◇ Nein, danke. Ich bin nicht durstig.
- ● Na gut, vielleicht ein andermal. Tschüß!

lange nicht gesehen	*long time no see*
zusammen	*together*
italienisch	*Italian food*
Lust haben zu	*feel like doing sth.*
mag mögen	*like*
nie	*never*
durstig	*thirsty*
na gut	*very well then*
vielleicht	*perhaps*
ein andermal	*another time*

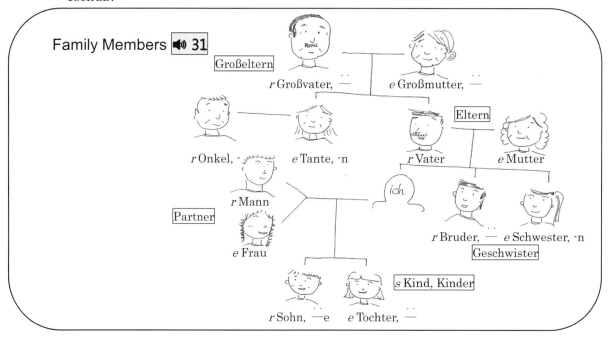

Family Members 🔊 31

Grammar 1 - *Der* Words

- A number of words used as articles before nouns take similar endings as definite articles; therefore, they are referred to as "*der* words." These are *dieser* (this / pl. these), *aller* (all), *jener* (that / pl. those), *solcher* (such), *jeder* (each, every), *mancher* (some, many a), and *welcher* (what, which). Their case forms are as follows:

	masculine	feminine	neuter	plural
nominative	dies**er**	dies**e**	dies**es**	dies**e**
genitive	dies**es**	dies**er**	dies**es**	dies**er**
dative	dies**em**	dies**er**	dies**em**	dies**en**
accusative	dies**en**	dies**e**	dies**es**	dies**e**

- Like the definite article, *der* words must agree in gender, number, and case with the nouns they precede. Note that this is similar to the English *this*, which also agrees with its noun, but only in number.

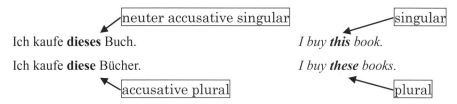

Ich kaufe **dieses** Buch.   I buy **this** book.
Ich kaufe **diese** Bücher.   I buy **these** books.

- The only exception to the declination pattern of definite articles (⇒ Lesson 2 Grammar 3) is in the neuter singular nominative and accusative, where the ending *-as* is replaced by *-es* (*das* - *dieses*).

German Proverbs – deutsche Sprichwörter (4)

Der Hunger kommt beim Essen.

Appetite comes with eating.

Lesson 6 - Invitations

Grammar 2 - *Ein* Words

- Similar to the *der* words (⇒ Grammar 1), a number of words used as articles before nouns take the same endings as indefinite articles; therefore, they are referred to as "*ein* words." *Ein* words are possessive adjectives (listed in the chart below), as well as the negative particle *kein*.

- As in English, every personal pronoun (*ich, du, er*, etc.) corresponds to a possessive adjective (*my, your, his*, etc.) indicating possession.

		personal pronouns		possessive adjective	
		English	German	English	German
singular	first person	I	ich	my	mein
	second person	you	du	your	dein
			Sie		Ihr
	third person	he	er	his	sein
		she	sie	her	ihr
		it	es	its	sein
plural	first person	we	wir	our	unser
	second person	you	ihr	your	euer
			Sie		Ihr
	third person	they	sie	their	ihr

- The endings of the *ein* words reflect the gender, number, and case of the noun modified. Their endings are identical to those for indefinite articles (⇒ Lesson 3 Grammar 2), and the endings for the plural forms are the same as the plural forms of the *der* words (⇒ Grammar 1).

	masculine	feminine	neuter	plural
nominative	mein	meine	mein	meine
genitive	mein**es**	mein**er**	mein**es**	mein**er**
dative	mein**em**	mein**er**	mein**em**	mein**en**
accusative	mein**en**	mein**e**	mein	mein**e**

- Note the difference from English, in which possessive adjectives do not vary by gender, number, or case.

    Das ist **mein** Vater. [masculine singular nominative]   *This is **my** father.*
    Das ist **meine** Mutter. [feminine singular nominative]   *This is **my** mother.*
    Das ist das Haus **meiner** Eltern. [plural genitive]   *This is the house of **my** parents.*

Grammar 3 - Negative Sentences Using *nicht* and *kein*

- In contrast to English, which uses *not* to negate affirmative sentences, German uses two separate words to negate sentences: *nicht* and *kein*.
- While *nicht* - like the English *not* - never changes in form, *kein* is an *ein* word that always agrees in gender, number, and case with the noun it modifies (⇒ Grammar 2).
- *Kein* is used to negate nouns preceded by indefinite articles or nouns without an article.

Ich habe ein Fahrrad.	*I have a bicycle.*
Ich habe **kein** Fahrrad.	*I don't have a bicycle.* [*I have no bicycle.*]

⟵ neuter singular accusative

Ich habe Geld.	*I have money.*
Ich habe **kein** Geld.	*I don't have money.* [*I have no money.*]

⟵ neuter singular accusative

- *Nicht*, however, is used to negate nouns preceded by a definite article, pronouns, adjectives, verbs, and other parts of speech. It is positioned after the verb, the subject, the direct object, and personal pronouns.

Ich kenne die Frau.	*I know the woman.*
Ich kenne die Frau **nicht**.	*I don't know the woman.*
Ich kenne sie.	*I know her.*
Ich kenne sie **nicht**.	*I don't know her.*
Sie ist schön.	*She is pretty.*
Sie ist **nicht** schön.	*She isn't pretty.*

- Do not confuse *nicht* (not) with *nichts* (nothing). *Nichts* represents a nominative or accusative complement.

Petra isst den Kuchen **nicht**.	*Petra **doesn't** eat the cake.*
Petra isst **nichts**.	*Petra **doesn't** eat **anything**.* [*Petra eats **nothing**.*]

Grammar 4 - Numbers 100 and Above

- Like their English counterparts, three- and four-digit numbers in German are read beginning with the hundreds and thousands.

  539   fünfhundertneununddreißig
  4325   viertausenddreihundertfünfundzwanzig

- Review the numerals from 0 to 100 (⇒ Lesson 3 Grammar 4) and familiarize yourself with the numbers 100 onward (⇒ Exercise 4).

Deutsch auf Englisch — Lesson 6 - Invitations

Exercise 1 【Grammar 1】
Fill the blanks with the correct *der* word endings.
① Welch____ Telefon gefällt dir besser, dies____ Smartphone oder jen____ Handy? *Which phone do you like better, this smartphone or that mobile phone?*
② Jed____ Japaner kennt dies____ Sängerin. *Every Japanese (r Japaner, -) knows this singer (e Sängerin, -innen).*
③ Nicht all____ Studenten sind fleißig. *Not all students (r Student, -en) are hard-working.*
④ An manch____ Tagen regnet es. *On some days (r Tag, -e) it rains.*

Exercise 2 【Grammar 2】
Fill the blanks with the appropriate possessive adjectives in their correct form to match the English translation. For the nouns expressing family relationship refer to the chart on ⇒ page 46.
① Die Schwester _____ Vaters ist _____ Tante. *The sister of my father is my aunt.*
② Der Sohn _____ Tante ist _____ Cousin. *The son of her aunt is her cousin.*
③ Zieht bitte _____ Jacken aus. *Please take off your (infml.) coats (e Jacke, -n).*
④ Machen Sie _____ Zigarette aus! *Put out your (fml.) cigarette (e Zigarette, -n)!*

Exercise 3 【Grammar 3】
Rewrite the following sentences as negative sentences using either *nicht* or the correct form of *kein*.
① Er hat heute Zeit. *He has time today.*
   → _____
② Dieses Buch ist interessant. *This book is interesting.*
   → _____
③ Ich kaufe dieses Auto. *I buy this car.*
   → _____
④ Ich kaufe einen Regenschirm. *I buy an umbrella.*
   → _____

Exercise 4 【Grammar 4】
Write out the following numbers in German words.
① 325   _____
② 839   _____
③ 4 353   _____
④ 73 322   _____
⑤ 590 117   _____

Deutsch auf Englisch — Lesson 6 - Invitations

Speaking Exercise 1 【Grammar 2】 🔊 32

Take turns with your partner asking each other about possessions and their price, as well as your opinion on the objects of everyday use depicted on ⇒ page 52. Exchange the underlined parts and pay extra attention to the correct form of indefinite articles, possessive adjectives, and *kein*, which are used both in nominative and accusative.

◇ Hast du einen Regenschirm?
Do you have an umbrella?

● Nein, ich habe keinen Regenschirm.
No, I don't have an umbrella.

● Ja, ich habe einen Regenschirm.
Yes, I have an umbrella.

◇ Wie viel kostet dein Regenschirm?
How much is your umbrella?

● Mein Regenschirm kostet 3 000 Yen. Wie findest du meinen Regenschirm? *My umbrella is 3.000 Yen. What do you think about my umbrella?*

◇ Ich finde deinen Regenschirm toll.
I think your umbrella is great.

++ toll *great*
++ super *fantastic*
+ schön *nice*
+ praktisch *useful*
+ preiswert *good value*
+- ganz nett *al'right*
- teuer *expensive*
-- schrecklich *terrible*
-- furchtbar *awful*

Speaking Exercise 2 【Grammar 3】 🔊 33

Practice inviting people and rejecting invitations with your partner. Use the pattern below and create dialogues for the activities shown in the pictures. For vocabulary, refer to ⇒ Lesson 4 Speaking Exercise (page 37).

● Hallo, Sebastian! Lange nicht gesehen! Fahren wir morgen zusammen Fahrrad?
Hello, Sebastian. Long time no see. Shall we go cycling together tomorrow?

◇ Nein, danke. Dazu habe ich keine Lust. Ich fahre nie Fahrrad.
No, thank you. I don't feel like doing that. I never ride a bicycle.

● Schade. Vielleicht ein andermal.
That's a pity. Perhaps another time.

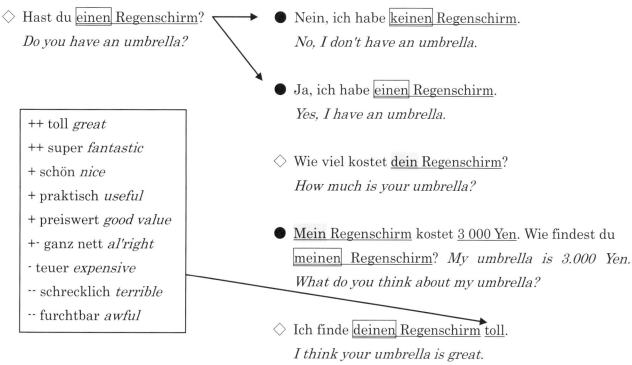

| example | ① | ② | ③ | ④ |

Deutsch auf Englisch

Lesson 6 - Invitations

Objectives

In this lesson you have learned how to

- ✓ use numerals over 100
- ✓ invite people and politely reject invitations
- ✓ express possession
- ✓ express likes and dislikes
- ✓ asking for and giving opinions

Vocabulary - Basic Nouns 4 🔊 34

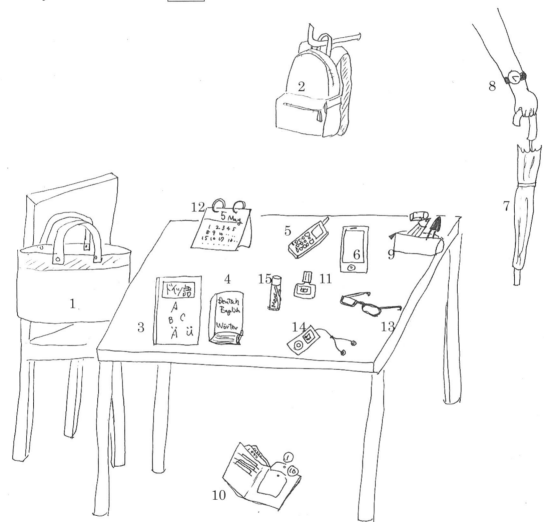

1 *e* Tasche, -n *bag*
2 *r* Rucksack, ⁻e *rucksack*
3 *s* Lehrbuch, ⁻er *textbook*
4 *s* Wörterbuch, ⁻er *dictionary*
5 *s* Handy, -s *mobile phone*
6 *s* Smartphone, -s *smartphone*
7 *r* Regenschirm, -e *umbrella*
8 *e* Uhr, -en *watch*
9 *s* Etui, -s *case*
10 *e* Geldbörse, -n *purse*
11 *pl.* Augentropfen *eye drops*
12 *r* Kalender, - *calendar*
13 *e* Brille, -n *glasses*
14 *r* MP3-Spieler, - *mp3-player*
15 *r* Lippenstift, -e *lipstick*

Lesson 7 - Visits

Dialogue - Darf ich dir etwas anbieten? 🔊 35

- Hallo Christian, darf ich hereinkommen?
- ◇ Hallo Andrea! Natürlich, bitte sehr! Darf ich dir etwas anbieten? Möchtest du einen Kaffee?
- Danke, sehr gern!

... einige Zeit später ...

- Christian, es tut mir leid, aber ich kann leider nicht länger bleiben. Ich muss morgen früh aufstehen.
- ◇ Schade. Musst du wirklich schon gehen?
- Ja, leider. Gute Nacht und bis bald!

herein|kommen *to come in* (verbs with separable prefixes ⇒ Lesson 8 Grammar 1)
natürlich *of course*
etwas *something*
an|bieten *to offer sb. sth.* (verbs with separable prefixes ⇒ Lesson 8 Grammar 1)
einige Zeit später *some time later*
es tut mir leid *I'm sorry (, but...)*
leider *unfortunately*
länger *longer* (comparative of *lang* (long) ⇒ Lesson 11 Grammar 2)
bleiben *to stay*
früh *early*
auf|stehen *to get up* (verbs with separable prefixes ⇒ Lesson 8 Grammar 1)
wirklich *really*
schon *already*
bis bald *see you soon*

Modal Verbs - Usefull Expressions 🔊 36

Soll ich ...? *Should I ...?*
  Soll ich die Tür schließen? *Should I close the door?*

Darf ich ...? *May I ...?*
  Darf ich Ihnen helfen? *May I help you?*

Wollen wir ...? *Let's...! / Shall we...?*
  Wollen wir zusammen Mittag essen? *Let's have lunch together! / Shall we have lunch together?*

Hier kann man ... *Here you can ...*
  Hier kann man die Fahrkarten kaufen. *Here you can buy the tickets.*

Hier darf man nicht ... *Here you are not allowed to ...*
  Hier darf man nicht rauchen. *You are not allowed to smoke here.*

Lesson 7 - Visits

Grammar 1 - Modal Verbs

- Like English, German uses modal verbs to express permission, ability, wants, necessity, obligation, or preferences.
- There are six modal verbs: *dürfen* (to be allowed to), *können* (to be able to), *mögen* (to like to), *müssen* (to have to), *sollen* (should), and *wollen* (to want to). In addition, *möchte*, the subjunctive II (⇒ Lesson 13 Grammar 1) of *mögen*, is used in a manner similar to modal verbs.
- The conjugation of modal verbs is irregular (irregular forms are underlined in the chart below) and should therefore be thoroughly memorized. Note that except in *sollen* and *möchte*, the stem vowels change in the singular forms (except for the *Sie* form). First and third person singular forms are identical.

	dürfen	können	mögen	müssen	sollen	wollen	möchte
ich	darf	kann	mag	muss	soll	will	möchte
du	darfst	kannst	magst	musst	sollst	willst	möchtest
Sie	dürfen	können	mögen	müssen	sollen	wollen	möchten
er / sie / es	darf	kann	mag	muss	soll	will	möchte
wir	dürfen	können	mögen	müssen	sollen	wollen	möchten
ihr	dürft	könnt	mögt	müsst	sollt	wollt	möchtet
Sie	dürfen	können	mögen	müssen	sollen	wollen	möchten
sie	dürfen	können	mögen	müssen	sollen	wollen	möchten

- Like their English counterparts, modal verbs in German are used in combination with a second verb (the main verb) in its uninflected form (the infinitive) to modify the latter's meaning. Unlike English, where the uninflected form is placed directly after the modal verb, a German modal verb (in normal declarative sentences), is placed in the second position of the sentence. The main verb will be positioned at the end of the sentence in its infinitive form. This is referred to as the *Satzklammer* (sentence brace) that frames the rest of the sentence.

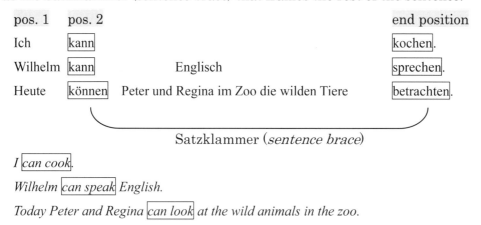

I can cook.
Wilhelm can speak English.
Today Peter and Regina can look at the wild animals in the zoo.

Lesson 7 - Visits

> Thoroughly familiarize yourself with the meaning and usage of each modal verb.

① **dürfen** *to be allowed / permitted to*

    Hier **darf** man rauchen.   *You are allowed to smoke here.*

    Hier **darf** man nicht parken.   *You are not allowed to park here.*

> A negated *dürfen* corresponds to the English "must not," expressing prohibition.

② **können** *to be able to, can*

    Meine Mutter **kann** gut kochen.   *My mother is good at cooking.*

③ **mögen** *to like to, may*

    Was **mag** das sein?   *What may this be?*

    Mögen Sie Rotwein?   *Do you like red wine?*

> If used without a main verb, *mögen* has the meaning of "to like."

④ **müssen** *to have to, must*

    Ich **muss** morgen arbeiten.   *I have to work tomorrow.*

    Du **musst** mir nicht helfen.   *You don't have to help me.*

> Unlike English, a negated *müssen* expresses the lack of necessity ("not have to do sth.").

⑤ **sollen** *should, is to, to be supposed to*

    Du **sollst** nicht lügen   *You should not tell a lie.*

⑥ **wollen** *to want to, to intend to*

    Meine Schwester **will** Lehrerin werden.   *My sister wants to become a teacher.*

> Be careful not to confuse the German *will* (first and third person of *wollen*) with the English modal verb *will*, expressing future prediction.

⑦ **möchte** *would like*

    Ich **möchte** einmal nach Japan [reisen].   *I would like to go to Japan once.*

    Ich **möchte** bitte ein Glas Bier [trinken].   *I would like a glass of beer please.*

> If the context is clear, *möchte* allows the omission of the main verb.

German Proverbs – deutsche Sprichwörter (5)

Steter Tropfen höhlt den Stein.

Constant dripping wears the stone.

Little strokes fell big oaks.

Deutsch auf Englisch — Lesson 7 - Visits

Grammar 2 - Future Tense

- As in English, future events or states can be expressed using a conjugated auxiliary verb and the infinitive of a main word. Similar to the use of modal verbs, German forms a sentence brace, placing the auxiliary verb *werden* (to become) in the second position with the infinitive of the main word positioned at the end of the sentence. This is different to English (where the auxiliary *will* is followed by the infinitive). Like modal verbs, *werden* appears in the first position in interrogative sentences without question words.

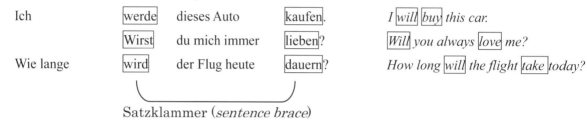

- *Werden* is an irregular, (e→i type) stem-vowel changing verb that should be memorized, since *werden*, together with *haben* and *sein*, comprise the most important irregular verbs in the German language (⇒ Lesson 2 Grammar 4).

infinitive	werden	
	singular	plural
first person	ich **werde**	wir **werden**
second person	du **wirst**	ihr **werdet**
	Sie **werden**	Sie **werden**
third person	er sie es } **wird**	sie **werden**

- Note that *werden* is also used as an auxiliary verb to form the passive (⇒ Lesson 12 Grammar 1).

- As introduced in ⇒ Lesson 2 Grammar 4, *werden* without an additional infinitival verb conveys the meaning *to become / will become*. It is used, for example, to describe a future desired profession or descriptions of future weather.

    Meine Tochter **wird** Polizistin. *My daughter will become a police officer.*
    Morgen **wird** es kalt. *It will be cold tomorrow.*

- In addition to the combination of *werden* + infinitive, German also expresses future concepts by using the present tense in combination with an adverb describing future time. This expression is more frequently used in German than in English.

    Ich fahre **nächste Woche** nach Amsterdam. *I will go to Amsterdam next week.*
    Bis Weihnachten sind wir wieder zu Hause. *We will be home by Christmas.*

Deutsch auf Englisch — Lesson 7 - Visits

Exercise 1 【Grammar 1】
Fill the blanks with the correct form of the modal verbs given in ( ).
① Du _____ nicht töten. (sollen) *You shall not murder.*
② Ich _____ einmal berühmt werden. (möchte) *I want to become famous someday.*
③ Wie lange _____ wir noch warten? (müssen) *How much longer do we have to wait?*
④ Du _____ mir nicht helfen. (müssen) *You don't need to help me.*
⑤ _____ ich Ihnen gratulieren? (dürfen) *May I congratulate you?*

Exercise 2 【Grammar 1,2】
Rewrite the following sentences using the modal verbs or *werden* given in ( ).
① Spielst du gut Volleyball? (können) *Are you good at playing volleyball?*
   → _____
② Günter sieht morgen den Film. (werden) *Günter will watch the movie tomorrow.*
   → _____
③ Wir rauchen nicht im Restaurant. (dürfen) *We don't smoke in the restaurant.*
   → _____
④ Der Lehrer kommt immer pünktlich zum Unterricht. (müssen) *The teacher is always on time for class.*
   → _____
⑤ Wir helfen anderen. (sollen) *We help others.*
   → _____

Exercise 3 【Grammar 1】
Translate the following sentences into German, using the correct modal verbs and the given vocabulary.
① Can Albert really speak Chinese? [wirklich   sprechen   Chinesisch]
   → _____
② The girl is allowed to go to the movies today. [s Mädchen   ins Kino gehen   heute]
   → _____
③ I want to eat icecream now. [essen   s Eis   jetzt]
   → _____
④ My brother has to get up at six o'clock every morning. [aufstehen   jeden Morgen]
   → _____
⑤ Shall we play Tennis together tomorrow? [Tennis spielen   zusammen   morgen]
   → _____

Deutsch auf Englisch — Lesson 7 - Visits

Speaking Exercise 1 【Grammar 1】 🔊 37

Talk with your partner about the following persons. Use modal verbs and *werden* as in the example below. Also pay attention to the correct forms of personal pronouns.

- ● Wer ist das? *Who is this?*
- ● Was **kann** er gut? *What is he good at?*
- ● Was **möchte** er machen? *What does he want to do?*
- ● Was **muss** er machen? *What does he have to do?*
- ● Was **wird** er in den Sommerferien machen?
  What is he going to do in the sommer holidays?

- ◇ Das ist Klaus.
- ◇ Er **kann** gut Motorrad fahren.
- ◇ Er **möchte** ein Motorrad kaufen.
- ◇ Er **muss** sparen.
- ◇ Er **wird** eine Spazierfahrt machen.

Name *name*	Klaus	Verena	Thomas und Birgit	Manuel
Fähigkeit *skill*	Er fährt gut Motorrad.	Sie spielt Geige.	Sie sprechen gut Französisch.	Er singt gut.
Wunsch *wish*	Er kauft ein Motorrad.	Sie sieht ein Konzert.	Sie machen eine Prüfung	Er wird ein Pop-Star.
Voraussetzung *prerequisite*	Er spart.	Sie kauft einen Fernseher.	Sie studieren fleißig.	Er lernt tanzen.
Plan für die Sommerferien *plan for the sommer holidays*	Er macht eine Spazierfahrt.	Sie übt jeden Tag Geige.	Sie fahren nach Frankreich.	Er geht oft in eine Karaoke-Bar.

---

kaufen *to buy*   **sparen** *to save / put away*   *e* **Spazierfahrt, -en** *drive*   *e* **Geige, -n** *violin*   *s* **Konzert, -e** *concert*   **üben** *practice*   **jeden Tag** *every day*   **studieren** *to study / to learn*   **fleißig** *hard working*   **tanzen** *to dance*   **oft** *often*   *e* **Karaoke-Bar, -s** *karaoke bar*

Deutsch auf Englisch — Lesson 7 - Visits

Speaking Exercise 2 【Grammar 1】

Practice inviting your partner using either one of the patterns and the vocabulary list below.

Pattern A 🔊 38

● Ich möchte dich <u>heute Abend</u> <u>zum Essen</u> einladen.   *I would like to invite you to dinner this evening.*

◇ Vielen Dank, aber leider kann ich nicht kommen.   *Thank you, but unfortunately I cannot come.*

● Schade.   *That's a pity.*

Pattern B 🔊 39

● Darf ich dich <u>heute Abend</u> <u>zum Essen</u> einladen?   *May I invite you to dinner this evening?*

◇ Gerne. Um wie viel Uhr darf ich kommen?   *I'd like to. At what time should I come?*

● Komm doch so um <u>drei</u>.   *Why don't you come around three o'clock?*

(← use an appropriate time)

---

example: **heute Abend / zum Essen**

① **morgen / zum Mittagessen**   *tomorrow / lunch*
② **am Wochenende / zu einer Spazierfahrt**   *weekend / drive*
③ **morgen Abend / zu einem Bier**   *tomorrow evening / beer*
④ **am Sonntag / zu Kaffee und Kuchen**   *Sunday / coffee and cake*
⑤ **übermorgen / zu mir**   *the day after tomorrow / my place*

German Proverbs – deutsche Sprichwörter (6)

Was Hänschen nicht lernt, lernt Hans nimmermehr.

You can't teach an old dog new tricks.

Deutsch auf Englisch

Lesson 7 - Visits

Objectives

In this lesson you have learned how to
- ✓ invite people and accept/reject invitations
- ✓ communicate during home visits
- ✓ express wants, preferences, necessity, ability, obligation, and permission
- ✓ talk about future events

Vocabulary - Basic Nouns 5 🔊 40

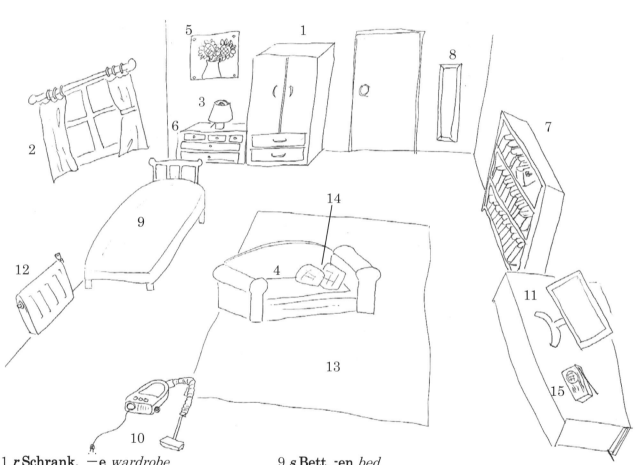

1 *r* Schrank, ¨-e *wardrobe*
2 *r* Vorhang, ¨-e *curtain*
3 *e* Lampe, -n *lamp*
4 *s* Sofa, -s *sofa*
5 *s* Bild, -er *picture*
6 *e* Kommode, -n *chest of drawers*
7 *s* Bücherregal, -e *bookshelf*
8 *r* Spiegel, - *mirror*
9 *s* Bett, -en *bed*
10 *r* Staubsauger, - *vacuum cleaner*
11 *r* Fernseher, - *TV*
12 *e* Heizung, -en *radiator*
13 *r* Teppich, -e *carpet*
14 *s* Kissen, - *cushion / pillow*
15 *s* Radio, -s *radio*

Lesson 8 - Health

Dialogue - Ich fühle mich schlecht. 🔊 41

- So, was fehlt Ihnen denn? Sie sehen ja gar nicht gut aus.
- ◇ Ich fühle mich auch schlecht. Mein Hals tut mir weh und ich habe Husten. Außerdem habe ich Fieber und Kopfschmerzen.
- Zeigen Sie mir mal Ihre Zunge!
- ◇ Aaah!
- Danke. Ich glaube, Sie haben sich erkältet. Ich verschreibe Ihnen einige Medikamente. Gute Besserung!
- ◇ Vielen Dank.

> **Was fehlt Ihnen?** [doctor to patient:] *What's your problem today?*
> **aus|sehen** *to look*
> **gar nicht** *not at all*
> **sich⁴ fühlen** *to feel sick*
> **sich³ weh|tun** *to hurt, to ache*
> **s Fieber** *fever, temperature*
> **außerdem** *besides, as well*
> **r Husten** *cough*
> **pl. …schmerzen** *pain, ache*
> **mal** [softening the imperative that would otherwise sound too much like an order]
> **glauben** *to think, to believe*
> **sich⁴ erkälten** *to catch a cold*
> **verschreiben** *to prescribe*
> **einige einig** *some*
> **s Medikament, -e** *medicine*
> **Gute Besserung!** *Get well soon!*

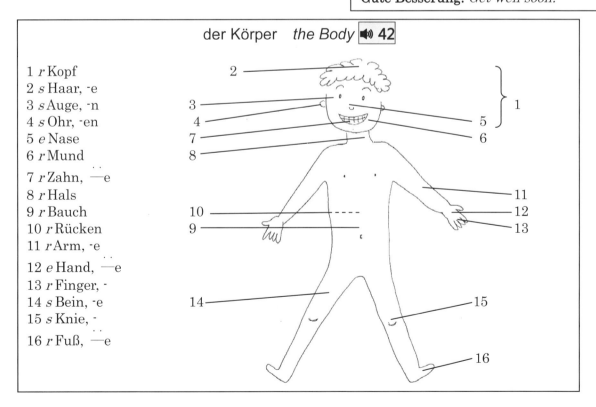

der Körper *the Body* 🔊 42

1 *r* Kopf
2 *s* Haar, -e
3 *s* Auge, -n
4 *s* Ohr, -en
5 *e* Nase
6 *r* Mund
7 *r* Zahn, ⁻e
8 *r* Hals
9 *r* Bauch
10 *r* Rücken
11 *r* Arm, -e
12 *e* Hand, ⁻e
13 *r* Finger, -
14 *s* Bein, -e
15 *s* Knie, -
16 *r* Fuß, ⁻e

Grammar 1 - Verbs with Separable Prefixes

- As in English, German uses prefixes to change the meaning of verbs.

  Ich schlafe. *I sleep.*

  Ich **ver**schlafe. *I oversleep.*

- In German, however, some prefixes added to verbs are separable. Verbs with such prefixes are therefore referred to as "separable verbs." This means that while the prefix is part of the infinitival verb form, it can be separated from the verb when the verb is conjugated. When separated, the conjugated verb (placed in second or first position depending on the type of sentence) and the separated prefix form a sentence brace framing the rest of the sentence.

infinitive:	aufstehen	*to get up*	
declarative sentence:	Ich	stehe	jeden Tag um 7 Uhr	auf.

  I get up every day at 7 o'clock.

interrogative sentence:	Wann	stehst	du jeden Tag	auf?

  At which time do you get up every day?

	Stehst	du jeden Tag um 7 Uhr	auf?

  Do you get up every day at 7 o'clock?

imperative sentence:	Steh	jeden Tag um 7 Uhr	auf!

  Get up every day at 7 o'clock.

  Satzklammer (*sentence brace*)

- Note that the prefix is not separated when these verbs appear with modal verbs (⇒ Lesson 7 Grammar 1) or in subordinate clauses (⇒ Lesson 9 Grammar 3).

  Ich muss jeden Tag um 7 Uhr **aufstehen**. *I have to get up every day at 7 o'clock.*

  Alle wissen, dass ich jeden Tag um 7 Uhr **aufstehe**.

  Everybody knows that I get up every day at 7 o'clock.

- Vocabularies and dictionaries commonly mark verbs with separable prefixes by placing a vertical line between the prefix and the infinitive (example: *auf|stehen*).

- The most common separable prefixes in German include the following: *ab-, an-, auf-, aus-, ein-, mit-, um-, vor-, weg-, zu-,* and *zurück-*. Since the meanings of separable verbs are commonly combinations of the original meaning of the verb and the meaning of the prefix, it is worth familiarizing oneself with the various meanings these prefixes may convey (example: *stehen* = to stand, *auf-* = on, on top of, up, open → *auf|stehen* = to stand up, to get up).

Deutsch auf Englisch | Lesson 8 - Health

Grammar 2 - Verbs with Inseparable Prefixes

➢ In addition to separable verbs, German also has "inseparable verbs," which have inseparable prefixes. In these verbs, the prefixes are never separated from the basic verbs; inseparable prefixes include *be-*, *emp-*, *ent-*, *er-*, *ge-*, *ver-*, and *zer-*.

infinitive:	besuchen	*to visit*
declarative sentence:	Ich besuche meine Eltern.	*I visit my parents.*
interrogative sentence:	Wann besuchst du deine Eltern?	*When will you visit your parents?*
	Besuchst du deine Eltern?	*Do you visit your parents?*
imperative sentence:	Besuch deine Eltern!	*Visit your parents.*

➢ Note that in separable verbs, the prefix is stressed, while inseparable prefixes are not.

    aúf|stehen   *besúchen*

➢ Some prefixes, such as *um-* or *über-*, can be either separable or inseparable, depending on their meaning and stress placement (that is, whether or not the prefix is stressed).

inseparable verb: umfáhren *to drive around*
    Das Auto umfährt die Katze. *The car drives around the cat.*

separable verb: úm|fahren *to run over*
    Das Auto fährt die Katze um. *The car runs over the cat.*

Grammar 3 - Reflexive Verbs

➢ Reflexive verbs (verbs accompanied by reflexive pronouns) are found in both English and German. The subjects and objects of these verbs refer to the same person or thing. In other words, the actions conveyed by these verbs are done to the subjects of their sentences.

    Ich wasche <u>mich</u>.   *I wash <u>myself</u>.*
    ↖ reflexive pronoun ↗

German Proverbs – deutsche Sprichwörter (7)

Des Teufels liebstes Möbelstück ist die lange Bank.

    literal translation: "The devil's favorite piece of furniture is the long bench." ("long bench" = idiom for procrastination → *Do not procrastinate!*)

- Like English, German has different reflexive pronouns for each person and number. In addition, German also distinguishes between the dative and accusative forms of reflexive pronouns in the first-person and second-person singular, these being identical to the corresponding personal pronouns (⇒ Lesson 4 Grammar 3). Note that in the third-person singular, one German pronoun (*sich*) corresponds to three different forms in English (*himself, herself, itself*). The formal *sich* is not capitalized.

			English	German	
				dative	accusative
singular	first person	(ich)	myself	mir	mich
	second person	(du)	yourself	dir (informal)	dich (informal)
		(Sie)		sich (formal)	
	third person	(er)	himself	sich	
		(sie)	herself		
		(es)	itself		
plural	first person	(wir)	ourselves	uns	
	second person	(ihr)	yourselves	euch	
		(Sie)		sich	
	third person	(sie)	themselves	sich	

- While many verbs can express reflexive meanings using reflexive pronouns, reflexive verbs in a stricter sense are those that obligatorily take either a dative or accusative reflexive pronoun. In vocabularies and dictionaries, reflexive verbs are often indicated by a preceding *sich*; datives or accusatives are shown by superscript numbers (*sich³* = dative, *sich⁴* = accusative).

infinitive	sich³ vor|stellen (*to imagine*)		sich⁴ erholen (*to relax*)	
	singular	plural	singular	plural
first person	ich stelle mir vor	wir stellen uns vor	ich erhole mich	wir erholen uns
second person	du stellst dir vor	ihr stellt euch vor	du erholst dich	ihr erholt euch
	Sie stellen sich vor		Sie erholen sich	
third person	er/sie/es stellt sich vor	sie stellen sich vor	er/sie/es erholt sich	sie erholen sich

- In German, reflexive pronouns are also used to express reciprocal actions, for which English uses *each other*.

    Wir werden uns immer lieben.   *We will always love each other.*

Deutsch auf Englisch — Lesson 8 - Health

Exercise 1 【Grammar 1】
Fill in the blanks with the correct parts of the verbs given in ( ).

① _____ du bitte das Fenster _____? (zu | machen)
   Could you close the window please?

② Das Flugzeug _____ um 10:30 Uhr _____. (ab | fliegen)
   The airplane will take off at 10:30 am.

③ Hoffentlich _____ du bald wieder _____! (zurück | kommen)
   I hope you will come back soon!

④ Wann _____ ihr jeden Morgen _____? (auf | stehen)
   At what time do you get up every morning?

⑤ Das Kind _____ vor dem großen Hund _____. (weg | laufen)
   The child is running away from the big dog.

Exercise 2 【Grammar 1】
Translate the following sentences into German using the vocabulary given in [ ].

① Many children watch TV every day. [viele Kinder, fern | sehen, jeden Tag]
   → _____

② He opens the door for the lady. [der Dame, auf | machen, die Tür]
   → _____

③ The marathon will take place tomorrow. [morgen, statt | finden, der Marathon]
   → _____

④ Will you call me tonight? [mich, an | rufen, heute Abend]
   → _____

⑤ Come with us! [mit uns, mit | kommen]
   → _____

Exercise 3 【Grammar 3】
Fill in the blanks with the correct <u>reflexive pronouns</u> and <u>reflexive verbs</u> given in ( ).

① _____ _____ nicht!
   Don't catch a cold. [informal *du* form] (sich⁴ erkälten)

② _____ du _____ immer die Hände vor dem Essen?
   Do you wash your hands every time before eating? (sich³ die Hände waschen)

③ Wir _____ _____ sehr.
   We love each other very much. (sich⁴ lieben)

④ Kannst du _____ ewigen Frieden _____?
   Can you imagine eternal peace? (sich³ vorstellen)

⑤ Ich _____ _____ sein Gesicht.
   I remember his face. (sich³ merken)

Deutsch auf Englisch — Lesson 8 - Health

Speaking Exercise 1 【Grammar 1】 🔊 43

Practice talking about pain in various parts of the body using the following dialogue and the parts of the body depicted in the pictures below.

- ● Was fehlt dir? — *What's wrong with you?*
- ◇ Ich habe [Knie]schmerzen. — *My knee aches.*
- ● Was tut dir weh? — *Where does it hurt?*
- ◇ Mir tut [mein Knie] weh. — *My knee aches.*

example	①	②	③	④	⑤

Speaking Exercise 2 【Grammar 1,3】 🔊 44

Talk to your partner about what you do after you return home every day. Pay attention to use the verbs with separable prefixes and reflexive verbs given below correctly. Use the informal expressions of time (⇒ Lesson 5 page 39).

- ● Wann kommst du nach Hause zurück? — *At what time do you return home?*
- ◇ Ich komme gegen <u>Viertel vor sieben</u> nach Hause zurück. Zuerst <u>wasche ich mir die Hände</u>. Dann _____ — *I return around a quarter to seven. First I wash my hands. Then ...*

zuerst *first,* **dann** *then,* **danach** *after that,* **zuletzt** *finally*

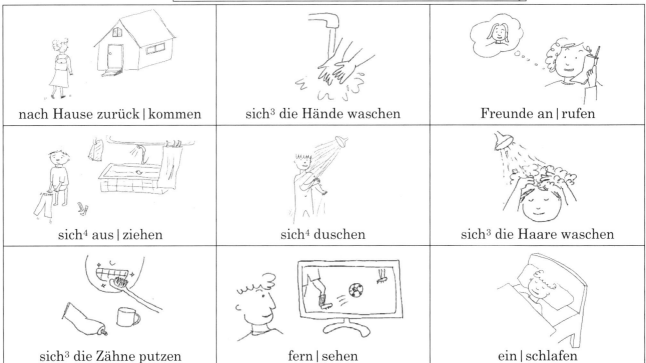

Deutsch auf Englisch   **Lesson 8 - Health**

Speaking Exercise 3 【Grammar 3】 🔊 45

Practice using reflexive verbs. Ask four of your classmates about their interests, pleasures, and anticipations etc., and write down their answers in the chart below.

- Worüber freust du dich?   ◇ Ich freue mich über das Geschenk.
- Worauf freust du dich?   ◇ Ich freue mich auf die Sommerferien.
- Wofür interessierst du dich? ◇ Ich interessiere mich für Volleyball.
- Worüber ärgerst du dich?   ◇ Ich ärgere mich über meine Lehrerin.
- Worauf bereitest du dich vor? ◇ Ich bereite mich auf die Prüfung vor.

combination of what + preposition (*wo*-compound ⇒ Supplement 3)

reflexive pronouns, accusative

direct object, accusative

Name	(example)				
Worüber freust du dich? *What are you pleased with?*	Geschenk *present*				
Worauf freust du dich? *What are you looking forward to?*	Sommerferien *sommer holidays*				
Wofür interessierst du dich? *What are you interested in?*	Volleyball *volleyball*				
Worüber ärgerst du dich? *Who / what are you angry at / about?*	meine Lehrerin *my teacher*				
Worauf bereitest du dich vor? *What do you prepare yourself for?*	Prüfung *test*				

Useful Vocabulary

r **Blumenstrauß**, ⁻e *bouquet of flowers*, *r* **Sieg**, -e *victory*, *r* **Besuch**, -e *visit*, *s* ***Weihnachten**, - *Christmas*, *e* **Party**, -s *party*, *s* **Wochenende**, -n *weekend*, *e* ***Musik**, -en *music*, *e* ***Geschichte**, -n *history*, ***fremde Kulturen** *different cultures*, *r* ***Lärm** *noise*, ***Politiker** *politicians*, **das schlechte Wetter** *the bad weather*, *e* **Fahrprüfung**, -en *driving test*, *s* **Date**, -s *date (a meeting with a person of the opposite sex)*, *r* **Wettkampf**, ⁻e *competition, contest*

words marked with * should be used without an article in this exercise

67 - siebenundsechzig

Deutsch auf Englisch

Lesson 8 - Health

Objectives

In this lesson you have learned how to
- ✓ communicate about health and sickness
- ✓ talk about illness and pain
- ✓ describe matters of daily routine
- ✓ express interest, pleasure, and anticipation

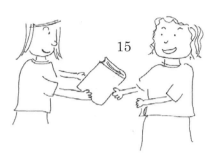

Vocabulary - Reflexive Verbs 🔊 46

1 sich⁴ **beeilen** *to hurry*
2 sich³ **weh tun** *to hurt oneself*
3 sich⁴ **erholen** *to relax*
4 sich³ etwas **vor|stellen** *to imagine sth.*
5 sich³ etwas **an|sehen** *to look at sth.*
6 sich⁴ **langweilen** *to be bored*
7 sich⁴ **verabschieden** *to say goodbye*
8 sich⁴ für etwas **interessieren** *to be interested in sth.*
9 sich⁴ **verlieben** *to fall in love*
10 sich⁴ **verletzen** *to injure oneself*
11 sich⁴ **aus|ruhen** *to have a rest*
12 sich³ *die Hände waschen* *to wash one's hands*
13 sich³ etwas **an|ziehen** *to put sth. on*
14 sich⁴ **unterhalten** *to talk, to converse*
15 sich⁴ **bedanken** *to express one's thanks*

Lesson 9 - Past Experience

Dialogue - Ich war schon einmal in Frankreich. 🔊 47

- ● Warst du schon einmal im Ausland?
- ◇ Nein, leider noch nie, da meine Eltern früher sehr streng waren. Ich durfte nicht ohne sie verreisen. Und du?
- ● Ich war schon einmal in Frankreich.
- ◇ Wie lange?
- ● Zwei Wochen, in Paris.
- ◇ Toll, da hattest du sicher viel Spaß!
- ● Ja, das war eine tolle Erfahrung, weil ich viele neue Leute kennenlernen konnte.

schon einmal *before*
***s* Ausland** *foreign countries*
noch nie *never before*
***pl.* Eltern** *parents*
früher *formerly, before*
streng *strict*
verreisen *to travel, to go away*
toll *great, fantastic*
sicher *certainly, surely*
Spaß haben *to enjoy*
***e* Erfahrung, -en** *experience*
neu *new*
***pl.* Leute** *people*
kennen|lernen *to get to know*

Expressions of Time Duration - **Wie lange?** *How long?* 🔊 48

r Tag, -e	drei Tage *three days*
e Woche, -n	zwei Wochen *two weeks*
r Monat, -e	sechs Monate *six months*
s Jahr, -e	ein Jahr *one year*

Wie lange warst du in Amerika? - Etwa drei Monate.
How long have you been in America? - About three months.

Wie lange möchtest du in Deutschland studieren? - Ein halbes Jahr.
How long do you want to study in Germany? - Half a year.

Lesson 9 - Past Experience

Grammar 1 - The Three Basic Verb Forms: Infinitive, Past, and Past Participle

> As in English, the main tenses for expressing past events or states in German are the simple past (*Präteritum*) and the present perfect (*Perfekt*). Before constructing these tenses, it is important to familiarize yourself with the various patterns of the three basic verb forms: infinitive, basic past form, and past participle. Also refer to the List of Common Irregular Verbs in the appendix (⇒ Appendix I) or consult your dictionary.

	infinitive	basic past form	past participle
regular verbs	—en	—te	ge—t
	lernen *to learn*	lernte	gelernt
irregular verbs I	—en	—*	ge—en [*]
	geben *to give*	gab	gegeben
	trinken *to drink*	trank	getrunken
irregular verbs II	—en*	—te*	ge—t*
	bringen *to bring*	brachte	gebracht
important verbs	**sein** *to be*	**war**	**gewesen**
	haben *to have*	**hatte**	**gehabt**
	werden *to become*	**wurde**	**geworden**
separable verbs	an|ziehen *to dress*	zog...an	angezogen
inseparable verbs	bekommen *to receive*	bekam	bekommen**
verbs ending in *-ieren*	studieren *to study*	studierte	studiert**

(* indicates stem-vowel change)

(** no prefix *ge-* is added)

> Note the stem-vowel change in irregular verbs, indicated by an * in the chart above. In some cases, the patterns of stem-vowel change in German verbs may resemble that of their English counterparts, e.g., *tr**i**nken* (to dr**i**nk) - *tr**a**nk* (dr**a**nk) - *getr**u**nken* (dr**u**nk) or *k**o**mmen* (to c**o**me) - *k**a**m* (c**a**me) - *gek**o**mmen* (c**o**me).

German Proverbs – deutsche Sprichwörter (8)

Ausnahmen bestätigen die Regel.

The exception that proves the rule.

Grammar 2 - Simple Past

> Like their English counterparts, German simple past verbs (*Präteritum* or *Imperfekt*) consist of one word. While the English simple past of regular verbs is constructed by adding *-(e)d* to the infinitive, *-te* is added to the stem of a verb to construct the simple past of German regular verbs.

infinitive:	lernen	*to learn*
stem:	lern	
simple past:	ich lernte	*I learned*

Like English irregular past forms, the past forms of irregular verbs in German include vowel changes or other spelling changes.

infinitive:	geben	*to give*
simple past:	ich gab	*I gave*

> While English uses only one verb form for the simple past, German simple past verbs are subject to conjugation, so change form according to the subject of the sentences in which they are used. This is done by adding further suffixes to the basic past form, e.g. (basic past form: *lernte*) *ich lernte* (I learned), *du lerntest* (you learned), *er/sie/es lernte* (he/she/it learned), *wir lernten* (we learned), *ihr lerntet* (you learned), and *sie lernten* (they learned).

		regular verbs	irregular verbs			
infinitive		lernen	gehen	sein	haben	werden
basic past form		lernte	ging	war	hatte	wurde
ich	—	lernte	ging	war	hatte	wurde
du	—st	lerntest	gingst	warst	hattest	wurdest
Sie	—(e)n	lernten	gingen	waren	hatten	wurden
er sie es	—	lernte	ging	war	hatte	wurde
wir	—(e)n	lernten	gingen	waren	hatten	wurden
ihr	—t	lerntet	gingt	wart	hattet	wurdet
Sie	—(e)n	lernten	gingen	waren	hatten	wurden
sie	—(e)n	lernten	gingen	waren	hatten	wurden

Note that in the first and third person singular, no additional ending is added; these forms are identical to the basic past form. The first- and third-person plural forms are identical.

> The simple past is mainly used in written texts, in storytelling or to refer to past events that have no strong relevance to the present. In spoken German, the simple past is also used for modal verbs, and for *sein* and *haben*.

Deutsch auf Englisch — Lesson 9 - Past Experience

Grammar 3 - Subordinating Conjunctions and Subordinate Clauses

- Like English, German has coordinating and subordinating conjunctions. While coordinating conjunctions such as *und* (and), *oder* (or), or *aber* (but) connect words or phrases of equal rank, such as two clauses, subordinating conjunctions introduce a subordinate clause (one that cannot stand alone and is dependent on the main clause). While coordinating conjunctions in English and German have no effect on word order, in German subordinating conjunctions introduce clauses in which the conjugated verb appears in the final clause position.

  coordinating conjunction: Es ist kalt und ich gehe nach Hause.   *It is cold and I go home.*
  subordinating conjunction: Ich gehe nach Hause, weil es kalt ist.   *I go home because it is cold.*

  normal word order = verb in the second position
  conjugated verb moved to the end of the subordinate clause
  [normal word order = verb in the second position: *Es ist kalt.*]

- A subordinate clause can be placed either before or after the main clause. If the subordinate clause precedes the main clause, the position of the conjugated verb in the following main clause moves to the beginning of the main clause. This positions the two conjugated verbs on either side of the comma.

  main clause→subordinate clause: Wir gehen zusammen ins Kino, sobald er nach Hause kommt.
  We will go to the movies together as soon as he comes home.
  subordinate clause→main clause: Sobald er nach Hause kommt, gehen wir zusammen ins Kino.
  As soon as he comes home we will go to the movies together.

- Another difference from English is the obligatory use of commas to separate subordinate and main clauses.

  Ich weiß nicht, wo er wohnt.   *I don't know where he lives.*
  Wo er wohnt, weiß ich nicht.   *Where he lives I don't know.*

- Make sure to memorize some of the most commonly used subordinating conjunctions.

① preceding a noun phrase	**dass** *that,* **ob** *if, whether*
② condition or time	**wenn** *if, when,* **als** *when,* **während** *while,* **bis** *until,* **seit/seitdem** *since,* **bevor/ehe** *before,* **nachdem** *after*
③ reason, cause	**weil** *because,* **da** *because, since*
④ purpose, aim	**damit** *so that*
⑤ result, consequence	**so dass** *so that*
⑥ concession	**obwohl** *although*

Deutsch auf Englisch

Lesson 9 - Past Experience

Exercise 1【Grammar 1】

Use your dictionary to find out the three basic forms of the following verbs.

infinitive	basic past form	past participle
spielen *to play*		
machen *to do*		
stehlen *to steal*		
telefonieren *to make a phone call*		
ein|kaufen *to shop*		
verkaufen *to sell*		
bringen *to bring*		
mit|bringen *to bring sth. with one*		
kochen *to cook*		
erleben *to experience*		

Exercise 2【Grammar 2】

Fill in the blanks with the correct past tense forms of the verbs given in ( ).

① Damals _____ wir noch in München. (wohnen) *We still lived in Munich at that time.*

② Vorhin _____ ich mich nicht gut. (fühlen) *A little while ago I didn't feel well.*

③ Davor _____ du Mathematik. (studieren) *Previously you studied mathematics.*

④ Letzte Woche _____ ihr jeden Tag zu mir. (kommen)
   You came every day to my place last week.

⑤ Vor 20 Jahren _____ ich noch in die Schule. (gehen) *I still went to school 20 years ago.*

Exercise 3【Grammar 3】

Connect the following sentences using the given conjunction. Pay attention to the correct position of the verbs.

① Ich kenne dich. Ich bin immer glücklich. *Since I got to know you I am always happy.*
   → Seitdem _____, _____.

② Du hörst nicht damit auf. Du wirst gefeuert. *If you don't stop it, you will be fired.*
   → Wenn _____, _____.

③ Kommen Sie bitte einmal in mein Büro. Sie fliegen ab. *Please drop by my office before you leave.*
   → _____, bevor _____.

④ Heute spielen wir Fußball. Es regnet stark. *Despite the heavy rain, we play soccer today.*
   → _____, obwohl _____.

⑤ Weißt du? Hat sie einen neuen Freund? *Do you know whether she has a new boyfriend?*
   → _____, ob _____.

Deutsch auf Englisch — Lesson 9 - Past Experience

Speaking Exercise 1 【Grammar 2】 🔊 49

Use the past tense to talk with your partner about your childhood memories. Ask each other about the topics in the chart below and note down the answers.

example: ◇ Was wolltest du werden? *What did you want to be?*
● Ich wollte Lokomotivführer werden. *I wanted to be an engine driver.*

	you	your partner
Was wolltest du werden? *What did you want to be?*		
Was durftest du nicht tun? *What were you not allowed to do?*		
Was musstest du tun? *What did you have to do?*		
Um wie viel Uhr musstest du ins Bett gehen? *At which time did you have to go to bed?*		

Speaking Exercise 2 【Grammar 3】 🔊 50

According to the example, complete the following sentences with information about your own habits and lifestyle and talk with your partner about it. Pay attention to the correct position of the verbs.

example: Wenn ich traurig bin, esse ich Schokolade. *When I am sad, I eat chocolate.*

① Wenn ich traurig bin,…   *When I am sad, ...*
② Ich bin sicher, dass…   *I am sure that ...*
③ …, weil ich keine Zeit habe.   *..., because I don't have time.*
④ Wenn ich Hunger habe,…   *When I am hungry, ...*
⑤ …, bevor ich schlafen gehe.   *..., before I go to sleep.*
⑥ …, wenn der Unterricht zu Ende ist. *..., when the classes are over.*
⑦ Seitdem ich Student/Studentin bin, … *Since I am a university student, ...*

Useful Vocabulary

Freunde anrufen *to call friends*   **sich⁴ zurück|ziehen** *to retire / retreat*   **die Prüfung bestehen** *to pass the exam*   **den Zug noch erreichen** *still catch the train*   **nicht so viel lernen können** *not be able to study so much*   **heute nicht mit|kommen** *don't come today*   **essen gehen** *to go out eating*   **etwas lesen** *to read something*   **ein Glas Bier trinken** *to drink a glas of beer*   **eine Zigarette rauchen** *to smoke a cigarette*   **joggen gehen** *to go jogging*   **viele neue Freunde haben** *to have many new friends*

Deutsch auf Englisch

Lesson 9 - Past Experience

Objectives

In this lesson you have learned how to

✓ ask and explain about past experiences
✓ describe past events
✓ expressing reasons, results, cause, purpose, etc.

Vocabulary - Verbs with Separable Prefixes 🔊 51

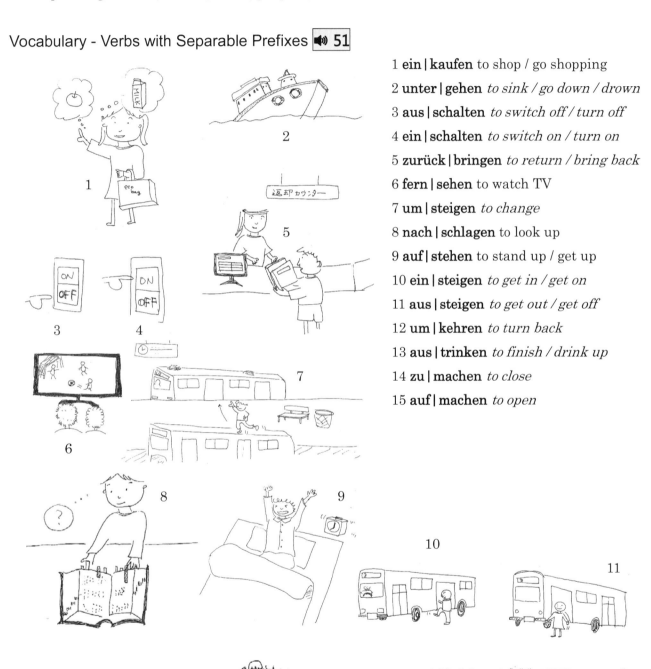

1 **ein|kaufen** to shop / go shopping
2 **unter|gehen** to sink / go down / drown
3 **aus|schalten** to switch off / turn off
4 **ein|schalten** to switch on / turn on
5 **zurück|bringen** to return / bring back
6 **fern|sehen** to watch TV
7 **um|steigen** to change
8 **nach|schlagen** to look up
9 **auf|stehen** to stand up / get up
10 **ein|steigen** to get in / get on
11 **aus|steigen** to get out / get off
12 **um|kehren** to turn back
13 **aus|trinken** to finish / drink up
14 **zu|machen** to close
15 **auf|machen** to open

Lesson 10 - Recent Events

Dialogue - Ich bin nach Japan geflogen.

- ● Was hast du denn eigentlich in den Sommerferien gemacht?
- ◇ Ich bin nach Japan geflogen. Zuerst war ich in Tokyo, dann in Kyoto und danach in Osaka. Zum Schluss bin ich bis nach Kyushu gefahren.
- ● Was hast du denn da alles gemacht?
- ◇ Ich habe z.B. das Nationalmuseum in Tokyo besichtigt und in Kyoto den „Goldenen Pavillon" angesehen. Außerdem habe ich auch das Schloss in Osaka besucht.
- ● Und wie war das Wetter?
- ◇ Erst war es sonnig, aber später hat es manchmal geregnet.

pl. **Sommerferien** *summer holidays*
geflogen [past participle of] **fliegen** *to fly*
zuerst *(at) first*
dann *then*
danach *after that, then*
zum Schluss *in the end, finally*
gefahren [past participle of] **fahren** *to go, to travel*
z.B. = zum Beispiel *e.g., for example*
s **Nationalmuseum, -seen** *national museum*
besichtigt [past participle of] **besichtigen** *to see the sights of ...*
r **„Goldener Pavillon"** *Temple of the Golden Pavilion Kinkaku-ji*
angesehen [past participle of] **an|sehen** *to look at*
s **Schloss, ¨er** *castle, palace*
besucht [past participle of] **besuchen** *to visit, to got o see ...*
s **Wetter** *weather*
erst *(at) first*
später *later*
geregnet [past participle of] **regnen** *to rain*

	Wie ist das Wetter?	Wie war das Wetter?
	Es ist sonnig.	Es war sonnig.
	Es regnet.	Es hat geregnet.
	Es schneit.	Es hat geschneit.
	Es ist heiß/warm/kalt.	Es war heiß/warm/kalt.
	Es blitzt und donnert.	Es hat geblitzt und gedonnert.

Deutsch auf Englisch — Lesson 10 - Recent Events

Grammar 1 - Present Perfect

➢ As in English, the present perfect (*Perfekt*) in German is formed by an auxiliary verb in the present tense and the past participle of the main verb. In German, however, these two parts of the present perfect form a sentence brace, with the conjugated auxiliary verb placed in the second position and the past participle at the end of declarative sentences.

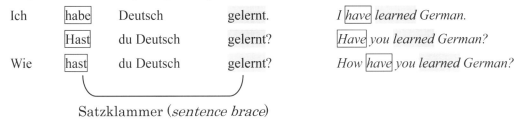

Ich	habe	Deutsch	gelernt.	*I have learned German.*
	Hast	du Deutsch	gelernt?	*Have you learned German?*
Wie	hast	du Deutsch	gelernt?	*How have you learned German?*

Satzklammer (*sentence brace*)

➢ Unlike English, which uses only *to have* as an auxiliary verb, the German present perfect requires either *haben* or *sein* as auxiliary.

| Er ist Anwalt geworden. | *He has become a lawyer.* |
| Er hat ein neues Auto gekauft. | *He has bought a new car.* |

Most verbs, including transitive, reflexive, and modal verbs, form the present perfect using the present tense of *haben* as an auxiliary verb. In the following cases, however, the present tense of *sein* is used instead.

①	intransitive verbs of movement	**gehen** *to go*, **kommen** *to come*, **fahren** *to drive*, **fallen** *to fall*, ...
②	intransitive verbs expressing change of state	**werden** *to become*, **sterben** *to die*, **auf|stehen** *to get up*, **ein|schlafen** *to fall asleep*, **passieren** *to happen*, ...
③	other intransitive verbs	**sein** *to be*, **bleiben** *to stay*, **begegnen** *to encounter*

It is thus advisable to memorize verbs together with the auxiliaries they use to form the present perfect. Your dictionary also provides this information, for example, by indicating the correct auxiliary by *h* or *s*.

➢ Note that German normally uses the present perfect in spoken language, with the simple past being more common in written language. Since the *Perfekt* is much more frequently used for expressing past in German than the present perfect is in English, the German *Perfekt* can often be translated using the English simple past. However, in German, the simple past is also used in conversation instead of the present perfect when the main verb is haben, sein, or a modal verb.

Jutta war schon einmal in Japan.	*Jutta has already been to Japan once.*
Gestern hatte ich keine Zeit.	*Yesterday, I didn't have time.*
Leider konnte mir niemand helfen.	*Unfortunately, nobody could help me.*

77 - siebenundsiebzig

Grammar 2 - Uses of *es* as a Subject

➤ *Es* (Engl.: *it*) functions as a personal pronoun, and just like its English counterpart it is also used in a variety of expressions referring to weather and time. *Es* is also used for expressions of mood. In some of these cases, it is not translated literally.

① expressions of weather: Es regnet. *It's raining.*
   Es ist kalt heute. *It's cold today.*

② expressions of time: Wie spät ist es jetzt? *What time is it now?*
   Es ist fünf Uhr. *It's five o'clock.*

③ expressions of feelings or mood: Wie geht es Ihnen? *How are you doing?*
   (*How's it going with you?*)
   Danke, mir geht es sehr gut. *Thank you, I'm very well.*

④ idiomatic expressions: Im Zoo gibt es viele Tiere. *There are many animals in the zoo.*

Grammar 3 - Infinitives with *zu*

➤ The use of *zu* + infinitive in most cases corresponds to the English *to* + infinitive construction. In contrast to English, however, the German *zu* + infinitive construction is separated from the main clause with a comma, and *zu* is followed by the infinitive at the end of the clause.

Ich plane, nach Berlin zu fahren. *I'm planning to go to Berlin.*

➤ The *zu* infinitive of separable verbs (⇒ Lesson 8 Grammar 1) is formed by inserting *zu* between the prefix and the verb.

Er erlaubt mir, mitzukommen. *He allows me to come with him.*

➤ Infinitives with *zu* can function as a noun, an adjective, or (in combination with a preposition) as an adverb:

① The *zu* infinitive as a noun: The *zu* infinitive is used as a subject or object of a sentence.
   Es ist schwierig, Deutsch zu lernen. / Deutsch zu lernen ist schwierig. *It is hard to learn German.*

② The *zu* infinitive as an adjective: The *zu* infinitive modifies nouns or adjectives.
   Ich habe keine Lust, ins Kino zu gehen. *I don't feel like going to the movies.*

③ The *zu* infinitive as an adverb: The *zu* infinitive is used in combination with a preposition (**um...zu** *in order to*, **ohne...zu** *without*, **(an)statt...zu** *instead of*).
   Er fuhr nach Berlin, um Medizin zu studieren. *He went to Berlin to study medicine.*
   Sie ging, ohne mich zu fragen. *She went, without asking me.*
   Er liest die Zeitung, statt zu arbeiten. *He's reading the newspaper instead of working.*

Deutsch auf Englisch — Lesson 10 - Recent Events

Exercise 1 【Grammar 1】
Complete the sentences using the appropriate auxiliary verbs (*haben* or *sein*) in their correct forms.
① Gestern _____ ich mir ein neues Handy gekauft. *Yesterday I bought myself a new mobile phone.*
② Am Wochenende _____ meine Eltern zurückgekommen. *At the weekend, my parents came back.*
③ Tina _____ in die Stadt gefahren und _____ das Museum besucht. *Tina went downtown and visited the museum.*

Exercise 2 【Grammar 1】
Complete the sentences in the present perfect using the correct auxiliary verbs and past participles.
① _____ du diesen Roman schon _____? *Have you already read* (lesen) *this novel?*
② Wann _____ du heute _____? *At what time did you get up* (auf|stehen) *today?*
③ Herr Müller _____ um 7 Uhr _____ und _____ im Zug _____. *Mr. Müller left* (ab|fahren) *at 7 o'clock and ate* (essen) *in the train.*
④ _____ ihr Japanologie _____? *Did you study* (studieren) *Japanese studies?*

Exercise 3 【Grammar 2】
Translate the sentences into English. Make sure to interpret *es* correctly.
① Heute regnet es.
  → _____
② Dort spielt ein Mädchen. Es ist drei Jahre alt.
  → _____
③ Gibt es ein Problem?
  → _____
④ Das Flugzeug ist abgeflogen. Es wird in zwei Stunden ankommen.
  → _____

Exercise 4 【Grammar 3】
Follow the example and write sentences using *zu* and the infinitive.
example: wichtig / immer vorbereitet sein   *It is important to be always prepared.*
  → <u>Es ist wichtig, immer vorbereitet zu sein.</u>
① unnötig / sich Sorgen machen   *It isn't necessary to be worried.*
  → _____
② altmodisch / so denken   *It is old-fashioned to think that way.*
  → _____
③ interessant / eine neue Sprache lernen   *It is interesting to learn a new language.*
  → _____

Deutsch auf Englisch — Lesson 10 - Recent Events

Speaking Exercise 1 【Grammar 1】 🔊 54

Use the present perfect to talk with your partner about the activities of the persons depicted in the chart below. Make sure to use the right auxiliary verbs (*haben* or *sein*) in their correct forms as well as the correct past participles.

example:
- ● Was hat <u>Max</u> am Wochenende gemacht? *What did Max do on the weekend?*
- ◇ Am Samstag [ist] <u>er</u> auf eine Party [gegangen]. *On Saturday he went to a party.*
  Und am Sonntag [hat] <u>er</u> lange [geschlafen]. *And on Sunday, he sleept late.*

	Max	Christine	Gisela und Markus	Günter	you	your partner
Samstag	auf eine Party gehen *to go to a party*	Hausaufgaben machen *to do the homework*	ein|kaufen *to shop*	mit Freunden essen gehen *to go out for a meal with friends*		
Sonntag	lange schlafen *to sleep late*	nach Berlin fahren *to go to Berlin*	nichts Besonderes machen *to do nothing special*	fern|sehen *to watch TV*		

Speaking Exercise 2 【Grammar 3】 🔊 55

Talk to your partner about how you use your smartphones. Use infinitive phrases and the vocabulary given below.

example:
- ● Wozu benutzt du dein Smartphone? *What do you use your smartphone for?*
- ◇ Ich benutze es, um <u>im Internet zu surfen</u>. *I use it to surf the internet.*

Useful Vocabulary

① **Musik hören** *to listen to music*   ② **fern|sehen** *to watch TV*   ③ **fotografieren** *to take photographs*   ④ **Hausarbeiten schreiben** *to write reports*   ⑤ **Spiele spielen** *to play games*   ⑥ **telefonieren** *to make phone calls*

Deutsch auf Englisch   Lesson 10 - Recent Events

Objectives

In this lesson you have learned how to
- ✓ describe the weather
- ✓ talk about events in the recent past

Vocabulary - Basic Nouns 6 🔊 56

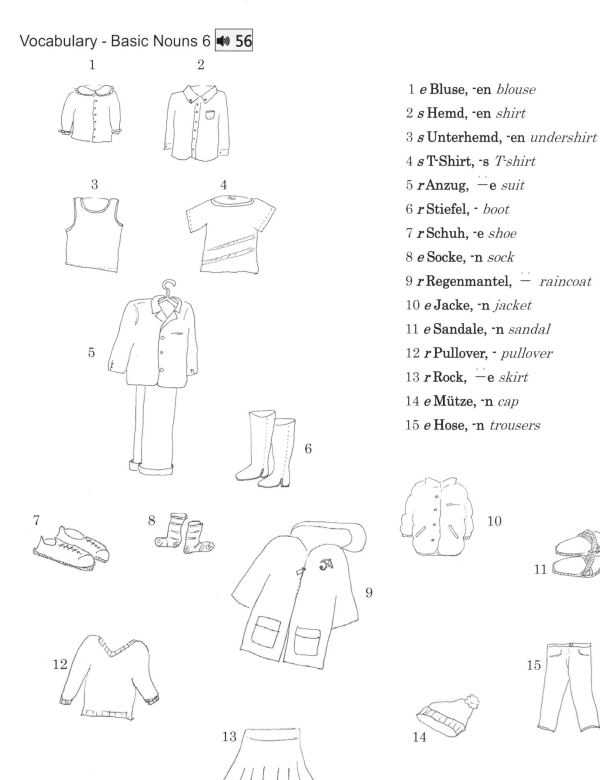

1 *e* Bluse, -en *blouse*
2 *s* Hemd, -en *shirt*
3 *s* Unterhemd, -en *undershirt*
4 *s* T-Shirt, -s *T-shirt*
5 *r* Anzug, ⁻e *suit*
6 *r* Stiefel, - *boot*
7 *r* Schuh, -e *shoe*
8 *e* Socke, -n *sock*
9 *r* Regenmantel, ⁻ *raincoat*
10 *e* Jacke, -n *jacket*
11 *e* Sandale, -n *sandal*
12 *r* Pullover, - *pullover*
13 *r* Rock, ⁻e *skirt*
14 *e* Mütze, -n *cap*
15 *e* Hose, -n *trousers*

Lesson 11 - Appearances

Dialogue - Tolle Party, nicht wahr? 🔊 57

- ● Tolle Party, nicht wahr? Sag mal, kennst du den jungen Mann dort drüben?
- ◇ Wen meinst du?
- ● Den attraktiven Mann in der schwarzen Jeans und mit dem gelben T-Shirt.
- ◇ Du meinst den Mann mit den langen braunen Haaren? Das ist Martin. Er ist sehr sportlich und viel netter als die anderen.
- ● Ich möchte ihn gerne kennenlernen. Aber ich glaube, er ist zu alt für mich.
- ◇ Nein, er ist kaum älter als du. Geh doch mal hinüber!

toll *great*
e Party, -s *party*
nicht wahr *isn't it?*
sag mal *(so) tell me, ...*
kennen *to know*
jung *young*
meinen *to mean*
e Jeans, - *jeans*
s T-Shirt, -s *T-shirt*
lang *long*
s Haar, -e *hair*
sportlich *sporty, athletic*
nett *nice, kind*
ander *other*
kennen|lernen *to get to know, to become acquainted with*
zu *too*
kaum *scarcely, hardly*
als *than*
doch *definitely*
hinüber|gehen *to go over*

Colors and Patterns 🔊 58

red	blue	green	yellow	flowered
rot	**blau**	**grün**	**gelb**	**geblümt**

brown	grey	white	black	striped
braun	**grau**	**weiß**	**schwarz**	**gestreift**

Deutsch auf Englisch — Lesson 11 - Appearances

Grammar 1 - Usage and Declension of Adjectives

- German adjectives can be used in three ways.
  - As in English, predicative adjectives in German are used with the verbs *sein* (to be), *bleiben* (to remain), or *werden* (to become) to describe subjects of sentences. The adjective follows the verb at the end of the sentence and does not vary in form, regardless of the gender or number of the subject.

Er ist faul.	*He is lazy.*
Die Kinder bleiben ruhig.	*The children remain calm.*
Die Wäsche wird trocken.	*The clothes become dry.*

  - In German, many adjectives can be used as adverbs, taking the same form. Such adjectives acting as adverbs modify verbs, other adverbs, or adjectives. Like predicative adjectives, they do not change their form but remain in the basic form listed in a dictionary without any additional endings.

Er schläft ruhig.	*He sleeps peacefully.*
Das Auto fährt langsam.	*The car drives slowly.*

  - As in English, attributive adjectives in German directly precede the nouns they describe. Unlike their English counterparts, German attributive adjectives change their forms to match a noun's gender, number, and case. In addition, the kind of article preceding the attributive adjective also determines the form of the adjective.

Er ist ein fauler Schüler.	*He is a lazy pupil.*
Das ist der faule Schüler.	*This is the lazy pupil.*
Ich schenke dem faulen Schüler ein Buch.	*I give a book to the lazy pupil.*
Das ist ein faules Mädchen.	*This is a lazy girl.*

- While predicative adjectives and adjectives as adverbs therefore do not change their forms, attributive adjectives (those used immediately in front of a noun) add endings to their basic forms to agree with the nouns they modify. They are declined for gender, number, and case. Furthermore, as shown in the chart on the next page, adjectives have three different patterns of endings depending on whether the adjective is preceded by a definite article or *der* word, an indefinite article or *ein* word, or by no article at all.

German Proverbs – deutsche Sprichwörter (9)

Wer rastet, der rostet.

A rolling stone gathers no moss.

	masculine	feminine	neuter	plural
① definite article or *der* word + adjective + noun				
nominative	der gute Mann	die gute Frau	das gute Kind	die guten Kinder
genitive	des guten Mann(e)s	der guten Frau	des guten Kind(e)s	der guten Kinder
dative	dem guten Mann	der guten Frau	dem guten Kind	den guten Kindern
accusative	den guten Mann	die gute Frau	das gute Kind	die guten Kinder
② indefinite article or *ein* word + adjective + noun				
nominative	ein guter Mann	eine gute Frau	ein gutes Kind	meine guten Kinder
genitive	eines guten Mann(e)s	einer guten Frau	eines guten Kind(e)s	meiner guten Kinder
dative	einem guten Mann	einer guten Frau	einem guten Kind	meinen guten Kindern
accusative	einen guten Mann	eine gute Frau	ein gutes Kind	meine guten Kinder
③ adjective + noun				
nominative	guter Mann	gute Frau	gutes Kind	gute Kinder
genitive	guten Mann(e)s	guter Frau	guten Kind(e)s	guter Kinder
dative	gutem Mann	guter Frau	gutem Kind	guten Kindern
accusative	guten Mann	gute Frau	gutes Kind	gute Kinder

Note that since there is no plural indefinite article, the possessive adjective (*ein* word) *mein* is used instead.

➢ Like their English counterparts, German adjectives can be turned into nouns. In German, adjectives used as nouns are capitalized and assigned a gender and corresponding adjectival ending appropriate for their context of use; these declensions follow the patterns explained above. If an adjectival noun refers to a person, German allows it to take not only the plural form but also, unlike English, the singular. The following sentences illustrate the usage of the adjective *krank* (ill, sick) as a noun. (see also ⇒ Supplement 4)

Der Arzt behandelt die Kranken.	*The doctor treats the sick.*
Der Kranke liegt im Bett.	*The sick man is in bed.*
Die Kranke liegt im Bett	*The sick woman is in bed.*
Ich pflege den Kranken.	*I nurse the sick man.*
Ich pflege die Kranke.	*I nurse the sick woman.*

Grammar 2 - Comparison of Adjectives

➢ Both English and German have two types of comparisons: the comparative and the superlative.

➢ The comparative of (regular) German adjectives is formed by adding *-er* to the basic form of the adjective, like the comparative of some English adjectives. However, in German, the stem vowels *a*, *o*, and *u* change into umlaut forms (*a→ä, o→ö,* or *u→ü*) if the adjective has only one syllable.

| schnell | → | schneller | *fast* | → | *faster* |
| lang | → | länger | *long* | → | *longer* |

Note that German does not have an equivalent to the English *more* comparative in which *more* appears with the basic form of the adjective. This construction is used in English with longer adjectives:

	interesting	→	*more interesting*		
	interessant	→	interessanter		

- German also shares with English the suffix *-st* to form the superlative of adjectives (*-est* after adjectives ending in *-t, -ß,* or *-sch*). For German superlatives, the stem vowels *a, o,* and *u* (of monosyllabic adjectives) are also changed into umlaut forms (*a→ä, o→ö,* or *u→ü*). German has no equivalent to the English superlative construction *most* + basic adjective.

schnell	→	schnellst	*fast*	→	*fastest*
lang	→	längst	*long*	→	*longest*
interessant	→	interessantest	*interesting*	→	*most interesting*

- Note that the superlative of predicative adjectives (⇒ Grammar 1) is formed by placing *am* before of the adjective and adding the ending *-(e)sten* to the adjective.

  Dieses Auto ist am schnellsten.   *This car is the fastest.*

- As in English, German has a number of adjectives with irregular forms in the comparative and the superlative. They should be memorized thoroughly. Some examples are given in the chart below.

	adjective (basic form)	comparative	superlative
		-er	-[e]st / am -[e]sten
regular	klein *small*	kleiner	kleinst / am kleinsten
	alt *old*	älter	ältest / am ältesten
partly irregular	groß *big, large*	größer	größt / am größten
	hoch *high, tall*	höher	höchst / am höchsten
irregular	gut *good*	besser	best / am besten
	viel *much, many*	mehr	meist / am meisten
	gern *[+verb] to like to do sth.*	lieber	liebst / am liebsten

- Note that in the case of attributive adjectives (adjectives used directly in front of the nouns they modify, ⇒ Grammar 1) the **adjective ending** is added after the comparative or superlative is formed.

  Der Fuji ist der höchste Berg Japans.   *Mount Fuji is the tallest mountain in Japan.*
  Ich möchte ein schnelleres Auto.   *I want a faster car.*

- Familiarize yourself with some of the most common sentence patterns for the basic form, the comparative, and the superlative of adjectives:
  - adjective (basic form)   Er ist so alt wie ich.   *He is as old as I am.*
    Er ist nicht so alt wie ich.   *He is not as old as I am.*
  - comparative
    Er ist drei Jahre jünger als ich.   *He is three years younger than me.*
  - superlative
    Er ist der faulste Schüler in der Klasse.   *He is the laziest pupil in the class.*
    Er ist am faulsten in der Klasse.   *He is the laziest in the class.*

Deutsch auf Englisch   Lesson 11 - Appearances

Exercise 1 【Grammar 1】
Fill in the blanks with the correct suffix of each adjective.
① Das war ein schön____ Abend! *This evening was nice (r Abend, -e).*
② Wo kann man diese lecker____ Würste kaufen? *Where can you buy these tasty sausages (e Wurst, ¨-e)?*
③ Die Tochter unseres streng____ Lehrers ist ein freundlich____ Mädchen. *The daughter of our strict teacher (r Lehrer, -) is a friendly girl (s Mädchen, -).*
④ Da ist gut____ Rat teuer. [saying] *It's hard to know what to do. (r Rat)*
⑤ Mit alt____ Freunden verbrachte ich eine angenehm____ Zeit. *I had a pleasant time (e Zeit, -en) with old friends (r Freund, -e).*

Exercise 2 【Grammar 2】
Fill in the blanks with the correct form of each adjective given in ( ). Use either the adjective in its basic form, the comparative or the superlative.
① Er ist nicht so _____ wie Albert Einstein. (intelligent) *He is not as intelligent as Albert Einstein.*
② Welches Zimmer ist am _____? (billig) *Which room is the cheapest?*
③ Der Audi ist _____ als dieser Volkswagen, aber der Mercedes ist am _____. (elegant [2x]) *The Audi is more elegant than this Volkswagen, but the Mercedes is the most elegant.*
④ Ich trinke Bier genauso _____ wie Wein. (gern) *I like to drink beer just as much as wine.*
⑤ Ist dein Bruder _____ oder _____ als du? (jung, alt) *Is your brother younger or older than you?*

Exercise 3 【Grammar 1,2】
Fill in the blanks with the correct form of each adjective given in ( ). Be aware that in addition to changing the adjectives into the comparative or superlative when necessary, also adjectival endings are required.
① Das ist das _____ Haus in der Umgebung. (groß) *This is the biggest house (s Haus, ¨-er) in the neighborhood.*
② Er ist mein _____ Freund. (gut) *He is my best friend (r Freund, -e).*
③ Haben Sie keine _____ Kleider? (preiswert) *Don't you have any dresses (s Kleid, -er) which are less expensive?*
④ Der _____ [Mensch] gibt nach. [saying] (klug) *Discretion is the better part of valor (r Mensch, -en).*
⑤ Claudia Schiffer ist die _____ Frau der Welt. (schön) *Claudia Schiffer is the prettiest woman (e Frau, -en) on earth.*

Deutsch auf Englisch Lesson 11 - Appearances

Speaking Exercise 1 【Grammar 1】 🔊 59

Practice using adjectives in a conversation between a customer and the staff at a department store.

- Guten Tag, ich suche ein T-Shirt. — *Hello, I'm looking for a T-shirt.*
  - [demonstrative pronoun, nominative] [indefinite article, accusative] [*der*-word, nominative]
- ◇ Wie gefällt Ihnen denn dieses rote T-Shirt? — *How about this red T-shirt here?*
- Das gefällt mir nicht so gut. Es ist zu altmodisch und nicht schick genug. Ich nehme lieber dieses blaue T-Shirt hier. — *I don't like it too much. It is too old-fashioned and not stylish enough. I prefer this blue T-shirt here.*
  - [personal pronoun, nominative] [*der*-word, accusative]

example	①	②	③	④

s T-Shirt	*r* Rock	*pl.* Schuhe	*e* Jacke	*s* Kleid
rot / blau	grün / grau	weiß / braun	schwarz / gelb	geblümt / gestreift
zu altmodisch *too old-fashioned*, nicht schick *not stylish*	zu kurz *too short*, nicht weit *not loose*	zu elegant *too elegant*, nicht praktisch *not convenient*	zu teuer *too expensive*, nicht sportlich *not sporty/casual*	zu eng *too tight*, nicht günstig *not at a good price*

German Proverbs – deutsche Sprichwörter (10)

Kleinvieh macht auch Mist.

A penny saved is a penny got.

Deutsch auf Englisch — Lesson 11 - Appearances

Speaking Exercise 2 【Grammar 2】 🔊 60

Talk to your partner about the persons depicted in the chart below. Use the basic form, the comparative and the superlative of the adjectives *alt* (old) – *jung* (young), *groß* (tall) – *klein* (short), *viel* (many) – *wenig* (few) to compare their age (*Alter*), height (*Größe*) and number of siblings (*Geschwister*).

- ● Wer ist am ältesten? — *Who is the oldest?*
- ◇ Alexander ist am ältesten. — *Alexander is the oldest.*
- ● Wer ist älter, Christine oder Thomas? — *Who is older, Christine or Thomas?*
- ◇ Christine ist älter als Thomas. — *Christine is older than Thomas.*
- ● Wer ist älter, Christine oder Paula? — *Who is older, Christine or Paula?*
- ◇ Christine ist genauso alt wie Paula. — *Christine is just as old as Paula.*

Thomas	Christine	Alexander	Paula
Alter: 16	Alter: 18	Alter: 23	Alter: 18
Größe: 170 cm	Größe: 170 cm	Größe: 180 cm	Größe: 185 cm
Geschwister: 3	Geschwister: 2	Geschwister: 0	Geschwister: 1

German Proverbs – deutsche Sprichwörter (11)

Übung macht den Meister.

Practice makes perfect.

Deutsch auf Englisch

Lesson 11 - Appearances

Objectives

In this lesson you have learned how to
- ✓ describe characteristics and appearances
- ✓ compare people and things
- ✓ express likes and dislikes

Vocabulary - Basic Adjectives 1

1 **voll** *full*
2 **leer** *empty*
3 **hart** *hard*
4 **weich** *soft*
5 **leicht** *light*
6 **schwer** *heavy*
7 **groß** *big, large*
8 **klein** *small, little*
9 **neu** *new*
10 **alt** *old*
11 **lang** *long*
12 **kurz** *short*
13 **billig** *cheap*
14 **teuer** *expensive*
15 **altmodisch** *old-fashioned*

89 - neunundachtzig

Lesson 12 - Procedures

Dialogue - Zuerst werden die Kartoffeln gekocht. 🔊 62

- ● Wie wird denn eigentlich ein deutscher Kartoffelsalat zubereitet?
- ◇ Also, zuerst werden die Kartoffeln gekocht und geschält.
- ● Und dann?
- ◇ Anschließend werden die Kartoffeln dann geschnitten, ebenso einige Zwiebeln und Gewürzgurken.
- ● Ist das alles?
- ◇ Nein, es werden noch Salz, Pfeffer, Kräuter und Öl dazugegeben. Zum Schluss muss noch alles vermischt werden.
- ● Danke, das werde ich einmal ausprobieren!

> *r* **Kartoffelsalat, -e** *potato salad*
> **zubereitet** [past participle of]
>   **zu|bereiten** *to cook, to prepare*
> **gekocht** [past participle of] **kochen** *to boil*
> **geschält** [past participle of] **schälen** *to peel, to skin*
> **anschließend** *after that, afterwards*
> **geschnitten** [past participle of]
>   **schneiden** *to chop, to slice*
> **ebenso** *in the same way, as well*
> **dazugegeben** [past participle of]
>   **dazu|geben** *to add*
> **zum Schluss** *finally, in the end*
> **noch** *on top of that, just*
> **vermischt** [past participle of]
>   **vermischen** *to mix, to blend*
> **aus|probieren** *to try out*

Zutaten für einen Kartoffelsalat *Ingredients for a Potato Salad* 🔊 63

e **Kartoffel, -n** *potato*
e **Gewürzgurke, -n** *pickled gherkin*
r **Pfeffer** *pepper*

e **Zwiebel, -n** *onion*
s **Salz** *salt*
pl. **Kräuter** *herbs*   *s* **Öl** *oil*

Deutsch auf Englisch — Lesson 12 - Procedures

Grammar 1 - Passive Voice

- Like English, German uses the past participle (⇒ Lesson 9 Grammar 1) of the main verb in combination with an auxiliary to construct passive sentences. However, while English requires a conjugated form of *to be*, the German passive is formed using *werden* (present tense ⇒ Lesson 2 Grammar 4, past tense ⇒ Lesson 9 Grammar 2) as an auxiliary. In passive constructions, auxiliary verbs and past participles form a sentence brace, similar to their patterning in the *Perfekt* (⇒ Lesson 10 Grammar 1).

    Dieses Buch wurde von ihm geschrieben.   *This book was written by him.*

    Satzklammer (*sentence brace*)

- Tense is indicated on the conjugated auxiliary *werden*. Note that in the present perfect, the past participle is formed without a preceding *ge-*: *worden*.

    present   Das Mädchen wird gelobt.   *The girl is being praised.*
    future   Das Mädchen wird gelobt werden.   *The girl will be praised.*
    simple past   Das Mädchen wurde gelobt.   *The girl was praised.*
    present perfect Das Mädchen ist gelobt worden.   *The girl has been praised.*

- When modal verbs appear in passive sentences, the infinitive *werden* appears at the end of the clause, and the modal verb takes the appropriate tense and agreement.

    present   Das Mädchen muss gelobt werden.   *The girl has to be praised.*
    simple past Das Mädchen musste gelobt werden. *The girl had to be praised.*

- Although the passive voice is frequently used when the agent (the performer of the action) is unknown, irrelevant, or omitted for other reasons, the agent can also be included in a passive sentence. While in English, such subjects are introduced by the preposition *by*, German uses either *von* + dative to introduce human agents or *durch* + accusative to introduce inanimate agents.

    Die Treppe wird jede Woche vom Hausmeister geputzt.   *The staircase is being cleaned every week by the janitor.*

    Das Haus wurde durch das Erbeben zerstört.   *The house was destroyed by the earthquake.*

- Transforming an active sentence into a passive one involves the procedure described below.
    1. The direct object (accusative) of the active sentence becomes the subject (nominative) of the passive sentence.
    2. The conjugated verb of the active sentence is changed into a past participle and moved to the end of the passive sentence. The appropriate conjugated form of *werden* is inserted to form a sentence brace.
    3. The subject (nominative) of the active sentence (the agent) is optionally introduced into the sentence by either *von* + dative case or *durch* + accusative case.

    Der Lehrer lobt das Mädchen.   *The teacher praises the girl.*

    Das Mädchen wird vom Lehrer gelobt.   *The girl is praised by the teacher.*

Grammar 2 - Stative Passive (*Zustandspassiv*)

➤ While the passive construction described above (also referred to as the dynamic passive) describes actions or events, the stative passive describes states or results. The stative passive resembles the dynamic passive in that it uses the past participle, but differs from it in its use of *sein* instead of *werden* as the auxiliary.

(dynamic) passive, present

Das Fenster wird geöffnet. *The window is being opened.*

(dynamic) passive, present perfect

Das Fenster ist geöffnet worden. *The window has been opened.*

stative passive

Das Fenster ist geöffnet. *The window has been opened.*
[literally: *The window is opened.*]

Grammar 3 - Relative Pronouns and Relative Clauses

➤ Like English, German uses the relative clause to describe people or things mentioned in the preceding sentence more precisely. For this purpose, both English and German use relative pronouns.

Das ist das Auto, [das] ich mir gestern gekauft habe.
     [relative pronoun]   relative clause

This is the car [that] I bought yesterday.

Note that in German, the relative clause is obligatorily separated from the main sentence by a comma or commas.

Das Auto, das ich mir gestern gekauft habe, ist teuer.
          relative clause

The car that I bought yesterday is expensive.

➤ While English uses different relative pronouns for persons and things (*who, which,* and *that*), German relative pronouns change their forms to agree with their precedents in gender, number, and case according to the following chart. German relative pronouns are identical to definite articles, with the exception of the highlighted forms.

➤

	masculine	feminine	neuter	plural
nominative	der	die	das	die
genitive	dessen	deren	dessen	deren
dative	dem	der	dem	denen
accusative	den	die	das	die

- The gender (masculine, feminine, or neuter) and number (singular or plural) of the relative pronoun are determined by the person or thing described more precisely in the relative clause, the antecedent. The case of the relative pronoun depends on which part of the relative clause is replaced by the relative pronoun. For example, if the relative pronoun replaces a direct object, the pronoun takes the accusative case. To determine the correct case, it can be helpful to rewrite the relative clause as an independent sentence to determine the function / case of the antecedent.

    Das Auto, das ich mir gestern gekauft habe, ist teuer.   *The car that I bought yesterday is expensive.*

    Relative pronouns agree with their **antecedents** in number and gender:
    das Auto → neuter, singular
    The function of the relative pronoun in the relative clause determines its case:
    Ich habe mir das Auto gestern gekauft. → direct object → accusative

- Note that relative clauses are subordinate clauses in which the conjugated verb appears at the end of the clause (⇒ Lesson 9 Grammar 3).
- Like their English counterparts, German relative pronouns can also be used in combination with prepositions. However, while **prepositions** in English relative clauses can appear in the final position, they always directly precede relative pronouns in German.

    Das ist die Kneipe, in die ich oft gehe.
    This is the bar [which] I often go to.

- Here are more examples showing the variety of German relative pronouns:

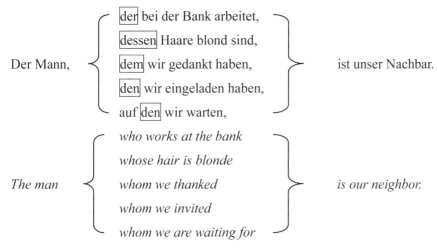

German Proverbs – deutsche Sprichwörter (12)

Der Teufel steckt im Detail.

The devil's in the detail.

Deutsch auf Englisch — Lesson 12 - Procedures

Exercise 1 【Grammar 1】
Fill in the blanks with the passive form in the present, past, or present perfect.

① Wann _____ das Gebäude morgens _____? (öffnen) *At which time does the building open in the morning?*

② Diese Dokumente _____ schon vor Jahren _____ _____? (zerstören) *These documents had already been destroyed years ago.*

③ Sie _____ von ihm nicht _____. (lieben) *She was not loved by him.*

④ Am Flughafen _____ das Gepäck _____. (kontrollieren) *At the airport, the luggage is checked.*

Exercise 2 【Grammar 1】
Rewrite the following sentences as passive sentences.

① Viele Touristen besuchen das Denkmal jedes Jahr. *Many tourists visit the monument every year.*
→ _____

② Der Polizist verhaftet den Einbrecher. *The policeman arrests the burglar.*
→ _____

③ Der Vater holt seine Tochter von der Schule ab. *The father picks up his daughter at the school.*
→ _____

④ Viele Menschen sahen diesen Film. *Many people watched this movie.*
→ _____

Exercise 3 【Grammar 3】 Fill in the correct relative pronouns.

① Der Computer, _____ ich mir gestern gekauft habe, ist schon kaputt. *The PC I bought yesterday is already broken.*

② Der Autor, _____ Roman ich gerade lese, ist schon gestorben. *The author whose novel I am reading at the moment is already dead.*

③ Das ist das Haus, in _____ wir wohnen. *This is the house we are living in.*

Exercise 4 【Grammar 3】
Use the appropriate relative pronouns to join the two given sentences so they match the English translations.

① Der Mann ist sehr klug. Der Mann ist Professor für Mathematik.
→ _____
The man, who is professor of mathematics, is very clever.

② Wie heißt der Film? In dem Film spielt Tom Cruise die Hauptrolle.
→ _____
What is the name of the film in which Tom Cruise plays the lead?

③ Kennst du das Buch? Der Autor des Buches hat den Nobelpreis erhalten.
→ _____
Do you know the book whose author won the Nobel Prize?

Deutsch auf Englisch — Lesson 12 - Procedures

Speaking Exercise 1 【Grammar 1,2】 🔊 64

Following the example, describe actions 1-4 listed in (a) row by forming sentences in the passive voice, and the resulting state listed in (b) row using the stative passive.

example) (a) Die Zwiebel wird geschält.
   (b) Die Zwiebel ist geschält.

	example	1	2	3	4
(a)					
(b)					
	die Zwiebel schälen *to peel the onion*	die Tür öffnen *to open the door*	eine E-Mail schreiben *to write an email*	den Tisch decken *to set the table*	das Auto waschen *to wash the car*

Speaking Exercise 2 【Grammar 3】 🔊 65

Using relative sentences, talk to your partner about famous places, sights etc. Make sure to use the correct relative pronouns and correct word order in the relative clauses.

example:

● Wie heißt das bekannte Schloss, das von König Ludwig II. erbaut wurde?
   What is the name of the famous castle build by King Ludwig II.?

◇ Das ist das Schloss Neuschwanstein.
   It is called Schloss Neuschwanstein.

example: das bekannte Schloss + das Schloss wurde von König Ludwig II. erbaut
1 das Tor in Berlin + das Tor ist ein Symbol für die Wiedervereinigung Deutschlands
2 die große Kirche + die Türme der Kirche sind 157 Meter hoch
3 das berühmte Bierfest + jedes Jahr nehmen über sechs Millionen Menschen an dem Bierfest teil
4 die alte Burg + in der alten Burg übersetzte Martin Luther das Neue Testament ins Deutsche

das Schloss Neuschwanstein, das Brandenburger Tor, der Kölner Dom, das Oktoberfest, die Wartburg

Deutsch auf Englisch

Lesson 12 - Procedures

Objectives

In this lesson you have learned how to

✓ understand and give descriptions of processes, procedures, etc. in the passive voice

✓ understand and use expressions of state by using the stative passive

✓ understand and construct sentences containing additional information on persons or things mentioned by using relative clauses

Vocabulary - Basic Nouns 7 🔊 66

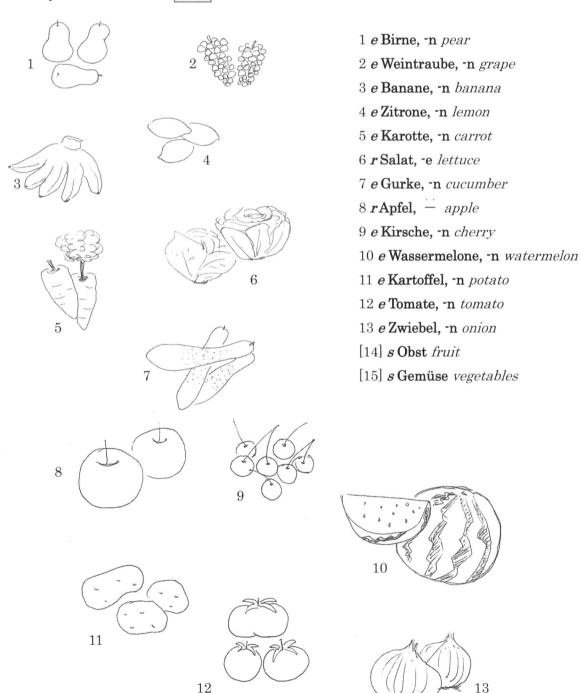

1 *e* Birne, -n *pear*
2 *e* Weintraube, -n *grape*
3 *e* Banane, -n *banana*
4 *e* Zitrone, -n *lemon*
5 *e* Karotte, -n *carrot*
6 *r* Salat, -e *lettuce*
7 *e* Gurke, -n *cucumber*
8 *r* Apfel, ¨ *apple*
9 *e* Kirsche, -n *cherry*
10 *e* Wassermelone, -n *watermelon*
11 *e* Kartoffel, -n *potato*
12 *e* Tomate, -n *tomato*
13 *e* Zwiebel, -n *onion*
[14] *s* Obst *fruit*
[15] *s* Gemüse *vegetables*

Lesson 13 - Dreams

Dialogue - Ach, wäre ich doch Millionär!
🔊 67

● Hast du schon gehört? Peter hat ein Stipendium für ein Studium in Japan bekommen!
◇ Toll! Ich würde auch gern in Japan studieren. Dann könnte ich jeden Tag viel Japanisch lernen und japanisch essen.
● Du hättest fleißiger lernen sollen! Dann hättest Du alle Prüfungen bestanden und auch ein Stipendium bekommen.
◇ Du hast ja Recht. Ach, wäre ich doch Millionär! Dann würde ich auch ohne Stipendium nach Japan fliegen.

s **Stipendium, -ien** *scholarship*
s **Studium, -ien** *study, study visit*
bekommen *[past participle of]*
    bekommen *to get, to receive*
studieren *to study*
s **Japanisch** *Japanese (language)*
japanisch essen *to eat Japanese food*
fleißiger *[comparative of]* **fleißig**
    hard-working, diligent
e **Prüfung, -en** *examination*
bestanden *[past participle of]*
    bestehen *to pass*
Recht haben *to be right*
ja *certainly*
doch *only* [emphasizes the
    (unrealizable) wish]
r **Millionär, -e** *millionaire*

Polite Requests - Frequent Patterns Using the Subjunctive II 🔊 68

Würden Sie ...? *Would you ...?*   Würden Sie mir Ihre Telefonnummer geben?
    Would you give me your telephone number?
Könnten Sie ...? *Could you ...?*   Könnten Sie das bitte noch einmal sagen?
    Could you say that again please?
Hätten Sie ...? *Would you happen to have ...?*
    Hätten Sie vielleicht morgen Abend Zeit?
    Would you happen to have time tomorrow evening?
Ich hätte ... *I would appreciate if you could ...*
    Ich hätte eine Bitte an Sie.
    Would you do me a favour?
Ich hätte gern ... *I would like to have ...*   Ich hätte gern ein Bier.
    I would like a beer please.
Dürfte ich ...? *May I ...?*   Dürfte ich Sie bitten, mir zu helfen?
    May I ask you for your help?
Könnte ich ...? *Could I ...?*   Könnte ich mitkommen?
    Could I come with you?

Lesson 13 - Dreams

Grammar 1 - Subjunctive II

- Like English, German expresses hypothetical conditions using verb forms based on the simple past tense. This mood is called subjunctive II (subjunctive I is used to express indirect speech; see ⇒ Supplement 8). Unlike English subjunctives, however, the German subjunctive II further modifies the simple past tense of irregular verbs by changing their stem vowels into umlaut forms and (in some cases) adding *-e* to the subjunctive endings.

    Ich wünschte, ich *hätte* ein Auto.
    I wish, I had a car.

- The (present) subjunctive II is constructed as shown in the chart below. For regular verbs, the simple past (indicative) and the subjunctive II are identical. For irregular verbs, also refer to your dictionary or the List of Common Irregular Verbs in the ⇒ Appendix I.

	regular verbs		irregular verbs (examples)			
infinitive	lernen		kommen	haben	werden	sein
basic past form	lernte		kam	hatte	wurde	war
ich	lernte	-[e]	käme	hätte	würde	wäre
du	lerntest	-[e]st	kämest	hättest	würdest	wär[e]st
Sie	lernten	-[e]n	kämen	hätten	würden	wären
er / sie / es	lernte	-[e]	käme	hätte	würde	wäre
wir	lernten	-[e]n	kämen	hätten	würden	wären
ihr	lerntet	-[e]t	kämet	hättet	würdet	wäret
Sie	lernten	-[e]n	kämen	hätten	würden	wären
sie	lernten	-[e]n	kämen	hätten	würden	wären

- Especially in spoken German, the subjunctive II of a verb is often replaced by the subjunctive II of *werden*, *würde*, in combination with the main verb in the infinitive. This resembles the English *would* + infinitive construction. Because this construction is often easier to form than the subjunctive II of verbs, it is advisable to familiarize yourself with it. Note, however, that this form of the subjunctive II is not used for *haben*, *sein*, or the modal verbs.

    Wenn ich die Prüfung bestünde, feierte ich eine große Party.
    Wenn ich die Prüfung bestehen würde, würde ich eine große Party feiern.
    If I passed the exam, I would give a big party.

- As in English, the German subjunctive II can also be used to refer to hypothetical conditions in the past. While English uses the past perfect, the German past subjunctive II is constructed using the *Perfekt* (auxiliary *sein* or *haben* + past participle), putting the auxiliary in the subjunctive II and changing the main verb into a past participle.

    present subjunctive II: Wenn ich sie liebte, heiratete ich sie.
    If I loved her, I would marry her.

    past subjunctive II: Wenn ich sie geliebt hätte, hätte ich sie geheiratet.
    If I had loved her, I would have married her.

- The subjunctive II is also used to form polite requests or ask for favors. Note the resemblance to polite requests in English with *would / could* + infinitive. For examples, refer to the frequently used patterns given on ⇒ page 97.

German Proverbs – deutsche Sprichwörter (13)

Was du heute kannst besorgen, das verschiebe nicht auf morgen.

literal translation: "Don't put off till tomorrow that which you can do today."

German Proverbs – deutsche Sprichwörter (14)

Alles hat ein Ende, nur die Wurst hat zwei.

literal translation: "All has an end, only a sausage has two ends." → *All things must come to an end.*

Deutsch auf Englisch — Lesson 13 - Dreams

Exercise 1 【Grammar 1】
Fill in the blanks with the correct forms (present subjunctive II) of the verbs given in ( ).

① Wenn ich mehr Zeit _____, _____ ich Spanisch lernen.
   If I had more time, I would learn Spanish. (haben, werden)

② Ich _____ ins Restaurant mitkommen, wenn ich jetzt Hunger _____.
   I would come with you to the restaurant if I were hungry now. (werden, haben)

③ _____ Sie mir sagen, wie ich zum Bahnhof komme?
   Could you tell me how to get to the station? (können)

④ Wenn ich du _____, _____ ich zu einem Rechtsanwalt.
   If I were you, I would to go a lawyer. (sein, gehen)

Exercise 2 【Grammar 1】
Fill in the blanks with the correct forms (past subjunctive II) of the verbs given in ( ).

① Wenn er gestern nicht so großen Durst _____ _____, _____ er nicht so viel _____. *If he hadn't been so thirsty yesterday, he wouldn't have drunk so much.* (haben, trinken)

② Wenn ich damals schon Englisch _____ _____, _____ ich nach Australien _____. *If I had been able to speak English at that time, I would have come with you to Australia.* (können · mit|fahren)

③ Wenn ich früher nettere Lehrer _____ _____, _____ mir die Schule mehr Spaß _____. *If I had had nicer teachers earlier, school would have been more fun for me.* (haben, machen)

④ Ich _____ [present subjunctive II] jetzt draußen Fußball spielen, wenn ich schon meine Hausaufgaben _____ _____. *I would be able to play soccer outside now, if I had done my homework already.* (können, machen)

Exercise 3 【Grammar 1】
Rewrite the following sentences in a more polite way using the subjunctive II.

① Kannst du mir bitte ein Bier geben?
   → _____

② Ich möchte gern ein Bier.
   → _____

③ Darf ich ein Bier haben?
   → _____

④ Gibst du mir bitte ein Bier?
   → _____

Deutsch auf Englisch — Lesson 13 - Dreams

Speaking Exercise 1 【Grammar 1】 🔊 69

Use the subjunctive II to talk to your partner about what you would do in the situations given below.

● Was würdest du machen, wenn du ein berühmter Popstar wärst?
   What would you do if you were a famous pop star?

◇ Wenn ich ein berühmter Popstar wäre, würde ich viele Mädchen kennenlernen.
   If I were a famous pop star, I would get to know many girls.

example: **Du bist ein berühmter Popstar.** *You are a famous pop star.*
1 **Du hast ein ganzes Jahr Ferien.** *You have a one year vacation.*
2 **Du bist Millionär.** *You are a millionaire.*
3 **Du bist Premierminister/-in von Japan.** *You are the prime minister of Japan.*
4 **Du triffst deinen Traummann / deine Traumfrau.** *You meet the perfect man/woman.*
5 **Du bestehst die Prüfung nicht.** *You fail your examinations.*
6 **Du kannst perfekt Deutsch sprechen.** *You speak perfect German.*

Useful Vocabulary

eine Weltreise machen *do a tour round the world*, **die gesammelten Werke Thomas Manns lesen** *read the collected works of Thomas Mann*, **einen Porsche kaufen** *buy a Porsche*, **allen meinen Freunden etwas schenken** *give something to all my friends*, **die Steuern senken** *lower the taxes*, **ihn/sie zum Abendessen einladen** *invite him/her to dinner*, **ihn/sie sofort heiraten** *marry him/her on the spot*, **noch fleißiger lernen** *study even harder*, **in Deutschland arbeiten** *work in Germany*, **Dolmetscher werden** *become an interpreter*

Speaking Exercise 2 【Grammar 1】 🔊 70

Rearrange the following sentences according to their level of politeness. Compare your findings with those of your partner and discuss the grammatical reasons for the different levels of politeness.

a) Können Sie mir bitte einmal das Salz geben?
b) Könnten Sie mir das Salz geben?
c) Salz!
d) Geben Sie mir bitte einmal das Salz?
e) Könnten Sie mir bitte einmal das Salz reichen?
f) Geben Sie mir das Salz!
g) Könnten Sie mir bitte einmal das Salz geben?

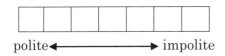

polite ← → impolite

Deutsch auf Englisch

Lesson 13 - Dreams

Objectives

In this lesson you have learned how to
- ✓ express hypothetical conditions or wishes
- ✓ make polite requests and ask favors

Vocabulary - Basic Adjectives 2 🔊 71

Draw pictures to illustrate the meaning of the following adjectives.

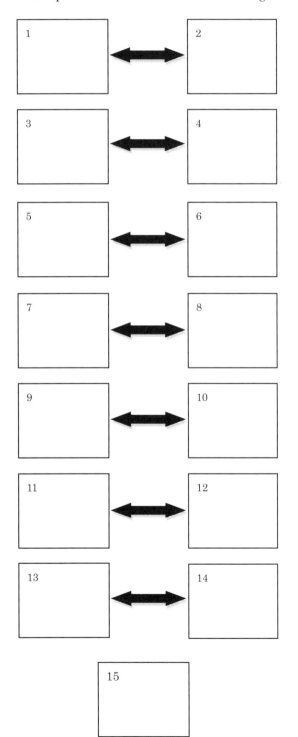

1 **laut** *loud*
2 **leise** *quiet*
3 **schön** *beautiful*
4 **hässlich** *ugly*
5 **gleich** *same, equal*
6 **unterschiedlich** *different*
7 **praktisch** *practical, useful*
8 **unpraktisch** *unpractical*
9 **zusammen** *together*
10 **allein** *alone*
11 **sauber** *clean*
12 **schmutzig** *dirty*
13 **freundlich** *friendly*
14 **unfreundlich** *unfriendly*
15 **cool** *coolly*

102 - hundertzwei

Supplement

Supplement 1 - Verbs: Present Tense (Regular Verbs) - Exceptions

➤ When the stem of a verb ends in -*d* or -*t*, an additional *-e* is added before the standard ending for *du*, *er/sie/es*, and *ihr*. Example: *arbeiten* [to work]; du arbeitest, er/sie/es arbeitet, ihr arbeitet

infinitive			arbeiten
stem			arbeit
singular		first person	ich arbeite
		second person	du arbeitest
			Sie arbeiten
		third person	er / sie / es arbeitet
plural		first person	wir arbeiten
		second person	ihr arbeitet
			Sie arbeiten
		third person	sie arbeiten

➤ When the stem of a verb ends in -*s*, -*ß*, -*ss*, -*tz*, or -*z*, the *du* form has the ending -*t* instead of the usual -*st* ending. Examples: *reisen* [to travel] → *du reist*; *benutzen* [to use] → *du benutzt*

Supplement 2 - Interrogative Pronouns *wer* and *was*

nominative	**wer**	who	**was**	what
genitive	**wessen**	whose	—	
dative	**wem**	whom	—	
accusative	**wen**	whom	**was**	what

Supplement 3 - Contraction of Prepositions and Interrogative Pronoun *was* (*Wo*-Compounds)

➤ When the interrogative pronoun *was* [what] is the object of a preposition, the so-called *wo*-compound is used. The prefix *wo-* (*wor-* if the preposition begins with a vowel) is added to the preposition. Examples: *mit was* → *womit*; *für was* → *wofür*

Supplement 4 - Adjectives as Nouns

> Adjectives can function as nouns. Adjectives used as nouns are capitalized and retain adjective endings according to which (understood) noun (for example, *Mann*, *Frau*, *Leute*, or *Ding*) they modify (⇒ Lesson 11 Grammar 1).

	singular		plural
	the sick person (masculine)	the sick person (feminine)	the sick
nominative	der Kranke	die Kranke	die Kranken
genitive	des Kranken	der Kranken	der Kranken
dative	dem Kranken	der Kranken	den Kranken
accusative	den Kranken	die Kranke	die Kranken

	neuter (singular only)
	the beautiful
nominative	das Schöne
genitive	des Schönen
dative	dem Schönen
accusative	das Schöne

Supplement 5 - Ordinal Numbers

> Ordinal numbers are created by adding *-t* to cardinal numbers up to 19 and *-st* to cardinal numbers 20 and up. When directly preceding a noun, adjective endings (⇒ Lesson 11 Grammar 1) must also be added to match the noun's gender, number, and case.

1. **erst**
2. zweit
3. **dritt**
4. viert
5. fünft
6. sechst
7. **sieb[en]t**
8. **acht**
9. neunt
10. zehnt
11. elft
19. neunzehnt
20. zwanzigst
24. vierundzwanzigst
100. hundertst

Supplement 6 - *Wer* and *was* as Relative Pronouns without Antecedents

> *Wer* and *was* as relative pronouns can be used without antecedents. They take the same forms as the interrogative pronouns (⇒ Supplement 2).

Wer	zuerst kommt, mahlt zuerst.	*First come, first served.*
Was	ich nicht weiß, macht mich nicht heiß.	*What you don't know won't hurt you.*
Das ist alles, was ich weiß.		*This is all I know.*

Deutsch auf Englisch — Supplement

Supplement 7 - Passive of Intransitive Verbs

➢ In contrast to English, German allows the use of intransitive verbs (verbs without an accusative object) in the passive voice. Since there is no reference to a personal subject (due to the lack of a direct object in the active voice), this form of passive is also referred to as "impersonal passive". The impersonal pronoun *es* is used as the formal subject of the sentence and is often omitted.

Er hilft mir.
He helps me. → Es wird mir geholfen.
　　　　　　　　　　Mir wird geholfen.

Man tanzt heute Abend.
Tonight there is dancing. → Es wird heute Abend getanzt.
　　　　　　　　　　　　　　Heute Abend wird getanzt.

Supplement 8 - Subjunctive I

➢ The subjunctive I is used for indirect speech. It is formed by adding the following endings to the verb stem:

		lernen	kommen	haben	werden	sein
ich	-e	lerne	komme	habe	werde	**sei**
du	-est	lernest	kommest	habest	werdest	**sei[e]st**
Sie	-en	lernen	kommen	haben	werden	seien
er / sie / es	-e	lerne	komme	habe	werde	**sei**
wir	-en	lernen	kommen	haben	werden	seien
ihr	-et	lernet	kommet	habet	werdet	seiet
Sie	-en	lernen	kommen	haben	werden	seien
sie	-en	lernen	kommen	haben	werden	seien

➢ Some examples:

Er sagt: „Ich bin krank."　　　　　　→　Er sagt, er **sei** krank.
He says, "I am sick."

Er fragte sie: „Wo wohnst du?"　　　→　Er fragte sie, <u>wo</u> sie **wohne**.
He asked her, "Where do you live?"

Er fragte mich: „Weißt du das nicht?"　→　Er fragte mich, <u>ob</u> ich das nicht **wisse**.
He asked me, "Don't you know that?"

Supplement 9 - Demonstrative Pronouns

- When used attributively, demonstrative pronouns take the same forms as the definite articles (⇒ Lesson 2 Grammar 3).

  das Buch da   *this book there*

- When used independently, demonstrative pronouns take the same forms as the relative pronouns (⇒ Lesson 12 Grammar 3).

  Kennst du den Mann dort?   Ja, **den** kenne ich.
  Do you know the man over there?   *Yes, I know him.*

- Note that demonstrative pronouns are often stressed and placed in the beginning of sentences.

Supplement 10 - Present Participle

- Present participles in German are formed by adding *-d* to the infinitive. When used directly preceding a noun, **adjective endings** (⇒ Lesson 11 Grammar 1) must also be added to match the noun's gender, number, and case.

  lachen *to laugh* → lachen**d** *laughing*

  ein **lachendes** Mädchen   *a laughing girl* [present participle as attributive adjective]

  Das Mädchen saß **lachend** da.   *The girl sat there laughing.* [present participle as adverb]

Supplement 11 - Expression of Years

- from 1100 to 1999: 1956 = neunzehn<u>hundert</u>sechsundfünfzig
- 1100 and before / 2000 and later: 2016 = zwei<u>tausend</u>sechzehn

---

German Proverbs – deutsche Sprichwörter (15)

Ende gut, alles gut.

All's well that ends well.

Appendix I - List of Common Irregular Verbs

infinitive	indicative present	indicative past (1st and 3rd person singular)	subjunctive II	past participle
bieten *to offer*		bot	böte	geboten
bleiben [s] *to stay, to remain*		blieb	bliebe	geblieben
bringen *to bring*		brachte	brächte	gebracht
denken *to think*		dachte	dächte	gedacht
dürfen *to be allowed to*	ich darf du darfst er/sei/es darf	durfte	dürfte	gedurft
essen *to eat*	du isst er/sie/es isst	aß	äße	gegessen
fahren [s] *to drive, to travel*	du fährst er/sie/es fährt	fuhr	führe	gefahren
fallen [s] *to fall*	du fällst er/sie/es fällt	fiel	fiele	gefallen
fangen *to catch*	du fängst er/sie/es fängt	fing	finge	gefangen
finden *to find*		fand	fände	gefunden
fliegen [s] *to fly*		flog	flöge	geflogen
fressen *to eat (animal)*	du frisst er/sie/es frisst	fraß	fräße	gefressen
gebären *to give birth to*		gebar	gebäre	geboren
geben *to give*	du gibst er/sie/es gibt	gab	gäbe	gegeben

Appendix I - List of Common Irregular Verbs

gehen [s] *to go*		**ging**	ginge	**gegangen**
gelten *to be valid*	du giltst er/sie/es gilt	**galt**	gälte / gölte	**gegolten**
genießen *to enjoy*		**genoss**	genösse	**genossen**
haben *to have*	ich habe du hast er/sie/es hat	**hatte**	hätte	**gehabt**
halten *to hold*	du hältst er/sie/es hält	**hielt**	hielte	**gehalten**
heißen *to be called*		**hieß**	hieße	**geheißen**
helfen *to help*	du hilfst er/sie/es hilft	**half**	hülfe	**geholfen**
kennen *to know*		**kannte**	kennte	**gekannt**
kommen [s] *to come*		**kam**	käme	**gekommen**
können *to be able to*	ich kann du kannst er/sie/es kann	**konnte**	könnte	**gekonnt**
laufen [s] *to run*	du läufst er/sie/es läuft	**lief**	liefe	**gelaufen**
lesen *to read*	du liest er/sie/es liest	**las**	läse	**gelesen**
liegen *to be lying down, to be situated*		**lag**	läge	**gelegen**
mögen *to like*	ich mag du magst er/sie/es mag	**mochte**	möchte	**gemocht**
müssen *to have to*	ich muss du musst er/sie/es muss	**musste**	müsste	**gemusst**
nehmen *to take*	du nimmst er/sie/es nimmt	**nahm**	nähme	**genommen**

Appendix I - List of Common Irregular Verbs

nennen *to name*		nannte	nennte	genannt
rennen [s] *to run*		rannte	rennte	gerannt
rufen *to call, to shout*		rief	riefe	gerufen
schaffen *to manage*		schuf	schüfe	geschaffen
schlafen *to sleep*	du schläfst er/sie/es schläft	schlief	schliefe	geschlafen
schlagen *to hit, to strike*	du schlägst er/sie/es schlägt	schlug	schlüge	geschlagen
schließen *to close*	du schließt er/sie/es schließt	schloss	schlösse	geschlossen
schneiden *to cut*		schnitt	schnitte	geschnitten
schreiben *to write*		schrieb	schriebe	geschrieben
schwimmen [s,h] *to swim*		schwamm	schwömme	geschwommen
sehen *to see*	du siehst er/sie/es sieht	sah	sähe	gesehen
sein [s] *to be*	[⇒ Lesson 1 Grammar 4]	war	wäre	gewesen
singen *to sing*		sang	sänge	gesungen
sitzen *to sit*	du sitzt er/sie/es sitzt	saß	säße	gesessen
sollen *to be obliged to*	ich soll du sollst er/sie/es soll	sollte	sollte	gesollt
sprechen *to speak*	du sprichst er/sie/es spricht	sprach	spräche	gesprochen
springen [s] *to jump*		sprang	spränge	gesprungen
stehen *to stand*		stand	stünde	gestanden
stehlen *to steal*	du stiehlst er/sie/es stiehlt	stahl	stähle	gestohlen

Appendix I - List of Common Irregular Verbs

steigen [s] *to climb, to rise*		**stieg**	stiege	**gestiegen**
sterben [s] *to die*	du stirbst er/sie/es stirbt	**starb**	stürbe	**gestorben**
tragen *to carry, to wear*	du trägst er/sie/es trägt	**trug**	trüge	**getragen**
treffen *to meet*	du triffst er/sie/es trifft	**traf**	träfe	**getroffen**
treten *to kick*	du trittst er/sie/es tritt	**trat**	träte	**getreten**
trinken *to drink*		**trank**	tränke	**getrunken**
tun *to do*		**tat**	täte	**getan**
vergessen *to forget*	du vergisst er/sie/es vergisst	**vergaß**	vergäße	**vergessen**
wachsen [s] *to grow*	du wächst er/sie/es wächst	**wuchs**	wüchse	**gewachsen**
waschen *to wash*	du wäschst er/sie/es wäscht	**wusch**	wüsche	**gewaschen**
werden [s] *to become*	du wirst er/sie/es wird	**wurde**	würde	**geworden (worden)**
werfen *to throw*	du wirfst er/sie/es wirft	**warf**	würfe	**geworfen**
wissen *to know*	ich weiß du weißt er/sie/es weiß	**wusste**	wüsste	**gewusst**
wollen *to want to*	ich will du willst er/sie/es will	**wollte**	wollte	**gewollt**
ziehen *to pull*		**zog**	zöge	**gezogen**

- ➤ [s] indicates verbs requiring *sein* as the auxiliary to form the *Perfekt*.
- ➤ This list includes the main irregular verbs used in the DIALOGUE and VOCABULARY section of each lesson. For more irregular verbs, refer to your dictionary.
- ➤ Separable / inseparable verbs are not listed.

Appendix II - List of Grammatical Terms

accusative	Akkusativ	対格　4格
active voice	Aktiv	能動態
adjective	Adjektiv	形容詞
adverb	Adverb	副詞
article	Artikel	冠詞
auxiliary verb	Hilfsverb	助動詞
cardinal number	Kardinalzahl	基数
case	Fall, Kasus	格
comparative	Komparativ	比較級
comparison	Komparation	比較
compound noun	zusammengesetztes Substantiv	複合名詞　合成名詞
conjugation	Konjugation	活用
conjunction	Konjunktion	接続詞
consonant	Konsonant	子音
coordinating conjunction	nebenordnende Konjunktion	並列の接続詞
dative	Dativ	与格　3格
declarative sentence	Aussagesatz	平叙文
declension	Deklination	語尾変化
definite article	bestimmter Artikel	定冠詞
demonstrative pronoun	Demonstrativpronomen	指示代名詞
der word		定冠詞類
diphthong	Diphthong, Doppellaut	二重母音
direct object	direktes Objekt	直接目的語
direct speech	direkte Rede	直接話法
ein word		不定冠詞類
feminine	feminin	女性の
future tense	Futur	未来形
gender	Genus, Geschlecht	性
genitive	Genitiv	所有格　2格
imperative	Imperativ	命令法

Appendix II - List of Grammatical Terms

indefinite article	unbestimmter Artikel	不定冠詞
indirect object	indirektes Objekt	間接目的語
indirect speech	indirekte Rede	間接話法
infinitive	Infinitiv	不定詞
inseparable verb	untrennbares Verb	非分離動詞
interrogative pronoun	Interrogativpronomen	疑問代名詞
interrogative sentence	Fragesatz	疑問文
intransitive verb	intransitives Verb	自動詞
irregular verb	unregelmäßiges Verb	不規則変化の動詞
main clause	Hauptsatz	主文
masculine	maskulin	男性の
modal verb	Modalverb	話法の助動詞
neuter	neutral	中性の
nominative	Nominativ	主格　1格
noun	Nomen, Substantiv	名詞
numeral	Zahlwort	数詞
object	Objekt	目的語
ordinal number	Ordinalzahl	序数
passive voice	Passiv	受動態
past participle	Partizip Perfekt	過去分詞
past tense	Präteritum, Imperfekt	過去形
personal pronoun	Personalpronomen	人称代名詞
plural	Plural, Mehrzahl	複数（形）
predicate	Prädikat	述語
prefix	Vorsilbe	接頭辞
preposition	Präposition	前置詞
present participle	Partizip Präsens	現在分詞
present perfect	Perfekt	現在完了形
present tense	Präsens	現在形
pronoun	Pronomen	代名詞
question word	Fragewort	疑問詞
reflexive pronoun	Reflexivpronomen	再帰代名詞
reflexive verb	reflexives Verb	再帰動詞
regular verb	regelmäßiges (schwaches) Verb	規則変化の動詞

Appendix II - List of Grammatical Terms

relative clause	Relativsatz	関係文
relative pronoun	Relativpronomen	関係代名詞
sentence brace	Satzklammer	枠構造
separable verb	trennbares Verb	分離動詞
singular	Singular, Einzahl	単数（形）
stative passive	Zustandspassiv	状態受動
stem	Stamm	語幹
stem vowel	Stammvokal	幹母音
subject	Subjekt	主語
subjunctive I	Konjunktiv I	接続法 I
subjunctive II	Konjunktiv II	接続法 II
subordinate clause	Nebensatz	従属節　副文
subordinating conjunction	unterordnende Konjunktion	従属の接続詞
suffix	Nachsilbe	接尾辞
superlative	Superlativ	最上級
syllable	Silbe	音節
three basic verb forms	Stammformen	三基本形
transitive verb	transitives Verb	他動詞
umlaut	Umlaut	ウムラウト
verb	Verb	動詞
vowel	Vokal	母音
weak noun	Substantiv auf -(e)n	男性弱変化名詞

Tobias Bauer（トビアス　バウアー）
熊本大学准教授

英語で学ぶドイツ語
Deutsch...
　　　...auf Englisch!

2017 年 3 月 1 日　初版発行　　定価 本体 2,200 円（税別）

著　者　© Tobias Bauer
発行者　近　藤　孝　夫
印刷所　萩原印刷株式会社
発行所　株式会社　同　学　社
〒112-0005　東京都文京区水道 1-10-7
電話 (03) 3816-7011(代)・振替 00150-7-166920

ISBN 978-4-8102-0888-7　　　　　　Printed in Japan

許可なく複製・転載すること並びに
部分的にもコピーすることを禁じます.